when a child
struggles in school

when a child struggles in school

everything parents + educators
should know about getting children
the help they need

Tom Jenkins, Ed.D.

Advantage

Published by Advantage, Charleston, South Carolina.
Member of Advantage Media Group.

ADVANTAGE is a registered trademark and the Advantage colophon is a trademark of Advantage Media Group, Inc.

Printed in the United States of America

ISBN: 978-1-59932-031-1
Library of Congress Control Number: 2006940047

Most Advantage Media Group titles are available at special quantity discounts for bulk purchases for sales promotions, premiums, fundraising, and educational use. Special versions or book excerpts can also be created to fit specific needs.

For more information, please write: Special Markets, Advantage Media Group, P.O. Box 272, Charleston, SC 29402 or call 1.866.775.1696.

table of contents

forward

This book was written for parents, by a parent. It could be characterized as "how to" advice on a subject of immense importance – your child's successful progress through school (and what to do when issues such as retention and special education eligibility/assessment become the focus of parent-teacher meetings). However, after completing this book, I realized that it is also for educators. It provides a clear and concise explanation of a better way to help children in need within an academic setting. So while this book seeks to empower parents, it also informs educators so that they can make good choices on how to go about meeting the needs of students.

Over many years of working with parents, teachers, and school administrators, I have witnessed firsthand what happens when a parent's anxiety and misunderstanding collides with federal, state, and school district regulations. The outcome of such collisions can sometimes lead to a loss of parent faith in the school district's decision-making. Likewise, the school district may have just created a long-standing headache for itself.

While the current federal regulations pertaining to special education services have not changed much regarding eligibility criteria since 1975 (Public Law 94-142, The Individuals with Disabilities Education Act), there is new hope. The "winds of change" are picking up speed and an alternative model for providing educational assistance to students in need is being recognized. This model, commonly referred to as Response to Intervention (RTI) could be good news for you and your child. How RTI could influence the choices you as a parent and your child's school have in meeting the educational needs of your child is the focus of this book. In this book you will read a lot about the results of implementation of a Response to Intervention model in school districts from North Carolina, South Carolina, and Virginia. However, these places are by no means the only places in which you could find a Response to Intervention model in place. In fact a Response to Intervention model has been in implementation the longest in the state of Iowa. School districts in Iowa began using Response to Intervention about 15 years ago, and it is now in use across the entire state. You can find a Response to Intervention model in several states. This past year at the national Response to Intervention conference, 20 different states were represented and two countries (New Zealand and Singapore). It just happens that I have been involved in implementation of a Response to Intervention model in NC, SC, and VA, so these implementation experiences are from where I draw the information that I will share with you in this book.

Keep in mind that the purpose of this book is to educate parents of students that are experiencing difficulties in school so that they might feel empowered to participate in the special education eligibility determination process and be advocates for what is best for their children. For that reason, I will attempt to make the research and implementation experiences as easy to understand as possible. This is not a meta-analysis, a research article, a technical journal, or a dissertation, and it will not be written as such. However, a list of relevant articles will be provided at the end of this book for those who wish to follow-up by reading the actual research articles discussed.

A glossary of terms is also provided at the end of this book. In the process of writing this book, I allowed several parents of students with disabilities to read the rough drafts to give me feedback. One idea that I consistently received from all was that it was difficult to remember acronyms and educational terms from one chapter to the next. Because of this, I have provided a quick reference list of terms, their acronyms, and their meanings. So as you read if you encounter a term or acronym that you do not remember, this list will be helpful.

I would like to make one final point about the book. In this book you will notice that I sometimes fluctuate between talking about students with learning disabilities and students receiving special education. This is an important thing to clarify. Students who are identified as having a learning disability are eligible to receive special education services. When the federal government created P.L. 94-142, or the Individuals with Disabilities in Education Act (IDEA), they generated different categories that students could fall into in order to be identified as a student with a disability and receive special education services. One of those categories is students with learning disabilities. When the federal government rewrote IDEA in 2005 they included Response to Intervention (RTI) as an option for school districts to use as a way of identifying students with learning disabilities. What you find through implementation of a Response to Intervention model is that you actually end up identifying students as eligible for special education services who previously would have fallen into categories such as learning disabled, other health impaired, developmentally delayed, educable mentally disabled, and behaviorally/emotionally disturbed. Even though the law is written for a RTI model to be used with students with learning disabilities, in actual implementation it can be used for all students with the mild disabilities previously listed. For that reason I sometimes talk about RTI with students with learning disabilities, and sometimes about RTI with special education students. This is not meant to be confusing, it is just the difference between the letter of the law and what actually happens during implementation.

ackNOWledgemeNts

Several people have influenced me during my career as an educator, but I would like to thank Ben Barbour for motivating and challenging me to do more and to be more. His efforts have had a profound impact on my life, and his collaboration had a significant effect on this book.

I wish to thank my parents for their unconditional love and support.

I thank my grandmother who was the first person in the family to have a book published.

I want to thank my children, Keir and Kyla, who constantly help me see the fun side of life. You put smiles on my face and love in my heart. I am so proud of both of you.

Finally, I thank my wife, Alethea for all of her support. You are my partner in life, my best friend, and my true love. It seems that we were made for each other. You are a wonderful wife and mother, and I appreciate your being the rock on which our family is built.

\|

the reasons

It all seemed to make sense. Or maybe it just seemed to make sense to me. I sat there explaining to a child's mother why her child could not have the help he so desperately needed. I explained that it was because of regulations. Regulations require that the child display a significant discrepancy between his IQ and his academic achievement scores. I explained that theoretically his IQ indicated his level of potential, and his academic achievement scores represented his actual level of performance. Because his IQ was in the low average range, his level of performance was consistent with his level of potential. Therefore, this child was not a student with a disability. Thus, he could not be given a label, nor could he receive special education services. This was despite the fact that he had repeated kindergarten and was now failing first grade. I went on to explain that perhaps if we tested him again later, in a year or so, he would display that ever-so-important discrepancy between his level of potential and his educational achievement. Perhaps then we could give him special education services. I knew my stuff. Not bad for a school psychologist fresh out of graduate school. I had read my texts. I had listened intently to my professors. I had successfully completed both my practicum and internship requirements. It seemed as though I was ready for anything anybody could throw at me. I seemed to have all of the answers, until I was asked two questions.

The first question came from the child's teacher. On the surface it seemed like a relatively easy question to answer, but it wasn't. After I had finished explaining why this child could not have the help he needed, she asked, "So what am I supposed to do with him?"

My initial response was to say the obvious, "Teach him." Then I realized that she did not know how to teach this child. This elaborate exercise that we had just completed, this expensive evaluation to determine special education eligibility, had told her nothing that had any instructional relevance. She had spent a few hours working with a team of people in the school deciding whether or not they should refer this child to me for this magical evaluation. Very little of that work she did with the team gave her the type of information she could use to go back and actually teach the child. Additionally, none of the standardized testing instruments used during the evaluation process gave her specific information on how to teach the child. Upon deeper inspection, this was a question that I could not answer, at least not working within this current evaluation system.

The second question was profound and came from the mother. It was one which I had not previously considered. None of my professors in graduate school had posed this question, and none of my textbooks mentioned it. The mother simply asked, "How many grades does my child have to fail before he can get the help he needs?" To this, there was obviously no answer. But, she had made her point. In the system in which I was working, this child would continue to fail until his performance was low enough that he could be identified as disabled, qualify for special education services, and get some help. The regulations, the system, and the special education evaluation process had failed that child. Worse, I had failed that child. The child was prevented from getting the help that he needed. Not only did he not receive special education services, but the process did not provide any information on how to teach him or help him be successful in his academic setting. Additionally, under the system in which I was working, "help" for this and other students was special education services. Why not get students the help they need without having to put a label on them, without having to put them in special education? Why can't we give them the academic help they need? Don't children deserve that?

I left that meeting thinking that there had to be a better way – a way to get children the academic assistance that they need sooner, a way to get children the academic assistance without their having to qualify for special education services, a way for them to get help without having to receive a label, and a way to help teachers understand how to teach children who are having difficulties. I don't remember the names from that meeting, but the lessons I learned that day are still with me. The process we used to evaluate children for special education eligibility, often referred to as the *discrepancy model,* does not work. And this scenario has played out countless times in American schools for the last thirty years. Countless children are being denied help. Countless parents are being told that there is nothing the school can do. Countless school psychologists, teachers, counselors, and principals are being left with a feeling that there must be something that can be done.

Numerous surveys have indicated that teachers, school psychologists, counselors, and other educational professionals feel that they were called to their professions out of their desire to help others. These "helping" professions have been caught up in an antiquated special education eligibility determination system which unintentionally finds itself promoting a "Wait to Fail" philosophy. Few things can be as frustrating to "helping" professionals as being placed in a systems breakdown which denies students early educational assistance because state and federal regulations imply that "this is the way we have always done it."

Well, there is something different that can be done. There is an alternative. This book is about my process of discovery. In the pages that follow I will explain the shortcomings of the discrepancy model and why it does <u>not</u> work. I will also explain an alternative process that is beginning to gain wide-spread support across America and is now included in the Federal regulations that govern special education, and under consideration for inclusion in the No Child Left Behind law. I will provide firsthand experiences, implementation stories from people in school settings, and explanations of research. My goal is for this book to be for people in and out of the field of education. But, this book is especially for parents because they are the advocates for their children. They are the ones who need to ask the important questions that bring about change. So, come take the journey with me.

2
how it all started

The federal government had good intentions when they passed Public Law 94-142, also know as the Individuals with Disabilities Education Act. In fact, in scope and intent, Public Law 94-142 was perhaps one of the top ten best pieces of legislation passed in the last century. The purpose was to make education more accessible to students with disabilities, and in this goal they were successful. The target population included, among others, students with learning disabilities (LD). In this law the federal government said that school districts needed to identify students with learning disabilities and provide them with "specially designed" services to promote successful learning. The problem came when the federal government never really reached consensus as to how school districts were supposed to identify these students with learning disabilities.

The first idea proposed was that assessments of students' mental processes could be performed, and these assessment results could be used to identify the students with learning disabilities. However, in 1975 when this law was passed, there was very little research regarding mental processes and even fewer tests that theoretically assessed these mental processes. So, the federal government was left in a quandary. How were they going to keep a cap on the number of students identified as having a learning disability? They decided to do just that, so they set a two percent cap on the number of students identified as having a learning disability. That is the way the law stood until just before it was passed, and at that time the idea of a discrepancy model was proposed. The basic premise of the discrepancy model is that if a student displays a significant difference between his level of potential or intellectual functioning (commonly associated with an IQ score), and his level of achievement, then theoretically he may be presumed to have a learning disability. Again, there was very little research regarding the validity of this theory, but there were IQ tests, and the theory seemed to make sense. The discrepancy model seemed like the best option at the time, and it gained plenty of support, so that was the method of identification that was adopted.

Since then, the research and practical implementation experiences have shown that there are lots of problems with IQ testing, achievement testing, and especially with the discrepancy model itself. When I think about this I am reminded of an analogy used by Dr. Ken Howell, a professor at Western Washington University: In Medieval times, a doctor would amputate a finger if it became infected. That was the widely accepted practice at the time; however, as medical knowledge and technology advanced, people improved ways to treat such ailments. In 1975 the discrepancy model was the accepted practice at the time; however, as our knowledge of children, education, learning, and assessment has advanced, we have become aware of better ways to identify and work with students with learning difficulties. If you went to a doctor today with an infection on your finger, would you accept a recommendation of amputation? If your child is recommended for evaluation to determine if he/she has a learning disability using the discrepancy model, should you accept the recommendation?

Before you answer, let's examine the issues surrounding IQ testing, achievement testing, and the discrepancy model.

3

what research and implementation experiences have taught us

Don't get me wrong. I see a lot of value in the services provided by special education programs. The original law (PL 94-142) has been expanded through a series of re-authorizations to include pre-school disabilities, students with autism, and other health-impaired individuals. The protection and expansion of disabled students' rights to a "free and appropriate public education" has increased dramatically since 1975. As satisfying as this progress is, the problem still lies in the way students are identified as eligible for special education services and the way the academic needs of students are identified and re-mediated. While I was working on a doctoral degree at the University of Virginia, a professor who was on my dissertation committee asked "what was wrong with special education?" This professor was a strong supporter of special education and believed in what it accomplishes for students. I responded that there is nothing wrong with special education, but if a student does not need it, why should he or she receive it?

Too many students are identified as eligible for special education and placed into special education programs who could have had their difficulties remediated in the general education setting with early intervention specific to their needs. This goes back to the issue that I brought up in the first chapter. Far too often "help" is conceptualized by educators as special education. Too many educators believe that a student can only receive the academic assistance that he needs if he is identified as a student with a learning disability. If the student needs help, why not just give him/her help? This would require implementation of a model in which interventions specific to student needs are provided in the general education setting. If these needs are met in the general education setting, consideration for special education services is not necessary.

Now let's get to the purpose of the next few chapters, examining the issues regarding IQ testing, achievement testing, and the discrepancy model. Before we get into what research and practical implementation have taught us, I want to explain how the process works. In a discrepancy model process, when a student is referred for special education eligibility consideration, the student is typically given an IQ test and an achievement test. The achievement test provides reading, math, and written expression scores. These scores are compared to the student's IQ score to determine if the student has a "significant" discrepancy. Discrepancy is another term for difference. Different states have different laws for what is a significant discrepancy, but most say somewhere between fifteen and twenty points. So if a student has an IQ score of 100 and a reading achievement score of 85, then there is a fifteen-point discrepancy. If the student lives in a state where a fifteen-point discrepancy is needed to be considered eligible for special education, then that student would be found eligible for special education as a student with a learning disability in the area of reading. If the student lives in a state where a twenty-point discrepancy is needed to be found eligible, then he would be found ineligible for special education services. At this point you are probably realizing one of the problems. Eligibility can depend upon where the student lives. But, let's save that for a later discussion, and first examine the issues regarding the use of IQ tests.

4
IQ tests

Theoretically, intelligence tests predict a student's ability to do well academically. Thus, when a student's IQ score is compared to an achievement score in search of a significant discrepancy, theoretically the school is comparing the student's *expected* level of performance to the student's *actual* level of achievement. However, the debate over whether IQ is even relevant when identifying a student with disabilities has raged for years.

The first argument is whether or not IQ tests actually measure intelligence. Intelligence is a theoretical construct. In other words, it is abstract. Yet this fact seems to be forgotten when it is being applied to the identification of students with disabilities. Analyses of IQ tests have shown that they measure such things as language skills, fine motor skills, specific knowledge of facts, and memory skills. Some argue that these things are neither the student's expected level of performance nor the student's level of potential; they are more concrete skills that can be affected by experiences and instruction. For this reason, some claim that IQ tests are actually achievement tests that measure past accomplishments. This is based on research that has shown that if a student has a learning disability, it is likely that his performance on an IQ test will be adversely affected. Additionally, instruction aimed at increasing the reading level of a student can lead to increases in the student's verbal scores on an IQ test. Experience with puzzles and computer games can lead to increases in the student's perceptual reasoning and processing speed scores on an IQ test. This is further supported by research findings that show if a student has a reading disability or language disorder, then that student's score on a language-based IQ test will be an underestimate of that student's ability to learn. It seems that IQ tests and achievement tests measure similar things, and perhaps comparing them in search of a discrepancy is, at a minimum, a questionable practice and is, at worst, a misleading practice.

A second criticism of IQ tests has to do with the notion that such tests are able to predict academic performance. Research has repeatedly shown the relationship between IQ test results and academic performance to be very weak. This is especially true when you compare the relationship of IQ tests and academic performance to the relationship of basic academic skills and more complex academic skills, such as knowledge of phonics and reading. Some research has even shown that IQ was useless when trying to predict which students had difficulty reading and which students were normal readers. IQ tests have been shown to be of limited value when trying to identify students already designated as impaired readers who were easy to remediate versus students already designated as impaired readers who were difficult to remediate. These results seem to be contrary to the idea that IQ tests are a reliable measure of the student's level of potential or the ability to do well academically.

A third area of contention regarding IQ tests is the belief that they are biased against minority students. This bias is believed to have caused an overrepresentation of minority students in special education classes. This overrepresentation is clearly evident in school districts across our nation. The Office of Civil Rights is a presence in these school districts telling them that they must do something to decrease the number of minority students in special education classes. Directors of special education programs are pulling their hair out trying to figure out a way to comply. The problem is that they are stuck using an eligibility determination system that is problematic. One study showed that in 46 of the 50 states the average percentage of minority students in classrooms for the mentally disabled was higher than the average percentage of white students in those same classrooms. Some argue that IQ tests are undoubtedly culturally biased because different students taking the tests have had different amounts of experience with the contents of the tests. Additionally, as Else Hamayan and Jack Damico pointed out in their book *Limiting Bias in the Assessment of Bilingual Students*, students from diverse cultures possess values, experiences, and cognitive and perceptual styles that can have adverse affects on their performance on assessments of intelligence. Hamayan and Damico further argued that the IQ assessment process requires that the student:

- have a formal relationship with the person administering the IQ test,

- possess thinking skills that are both analytical and reflective,

- value competition and have experiences in competitive situations,

- have experience and knowledge about taking tests that are standardized and timed,

- be familiar with and have experience in the content of the IQ test which is culturally influenced,

- possess a high degree of understanding and comfort with mainstream culture,

- and possess an understanding of the verbal and nonverbal communications inherent in the IQ assessment process.

Students from different cultural backgrounds usually are unable to satisfy these requirements. This creates bias in the assessment process and invalidates standardized test results. In the traditional IQ assessment process culturally diverse students are often inappropriately evaluated, and the results are used to identify the students as disabled.

5
achievement tests

In the discrepancy model there are two parts of the equation. The first is intelligence tests, which were covered in the previous chapter. The second part of the equation is represented by achievement tests. Achievement tests are not without criticism. Think about it logically. Achievement tests are built to measure the academic skills of students in grades kindergarten through twelve. Some even go as far as to attempt to measure academic skills through adulthood. How can one test, developed to be administered in about an hour and a half, be capable of effectively measuring all of the academic skills from kindergarten through twelfth grade – let alone adulthood? As a result, achievement tests are comprised of items that are not adequately representative of curriculum content. Rather, achievement tests measure chunks of curriculum that are too large, and thus are useless when trying to detect the effects of instruction. They lack specificity. They can provide a basic reading skill score or a reading comprehension skills score, but they cannot get any more specific than that. For example, they cannot provide a score for the component skills of reading such as letter identification skills, phoneme identification skills, phonological awareness skills, sight word skills, etc.

Since achievement tests lack that specificity, they are not sensitive enough to display progress that students show as a result of instruction over a short period of time. Research has shown that students can be given achievement tests, then those same achievement tests can be given to the students ten weeks later. Those achievement tests will show that the student's scores remain the same. This appears to indicate that the students made no progress, despite receiving instruction for those ten weeks. However, when more specific curriculum-based assessment instruments are used, the results indicate that the students made progress as a result of instruction. This eliminates achievement tests from being used for monitoring the academic progress of a student. Additionally, achievement test assessment procedures recommend that once a test is administered to a student, the same test not be given to that student again until at least six months later. This eliminates achievement tests from being used to progress monitor a student's response to instruction. Progress monitoring should occur at least on a weekly basis. The best practice is for progress monitoring to occur two to three times a week. Again, more specific curriculum based assessment instruments can be given with the frequency necessary to effectively progress monitor. Curriculum-based assessments require a significantly shorter administration time, which again makes them more appropriate for monitoring a student's progress. (Curriculum-based assessment tools will be discussed in a later chapter.)

In a discrepancy model, achievement tests are supposed to provide an indication of where the student is functioning academically. The theory is that teachers can take achievement test results and develop a plan of what and how to teach the student. Since achievement tests are inadequate in detecting the effects of instruction, they are also of limited usefulness when trying to develop an instructional plan for a student. It again boils down to the lack of specificity. An achievement test may tell you that the student's basic reading score is an 88. Unfortunately, that does not tell the teacher anything about the student's component skills of reading, so the teacher has no idea how or what to teach the student. It leaves the teacher wondering what specific component skills of reading the student has mastered. What specific component skills of reading need strengthening?

An additional problem in this area is that achievement tests are generic academic assessments, which means they are not connected to local curriculum. Most states have established curriculum expectations for each grade level. Curricula are specific to each state, and some are even specific to each school district. Because achievement tests are not connected to individual curricula, often skills that are believed to be expectations for particular grade levels on achievement tests are inappropriate expectations. Achievement test developers do not consider different curricula for different states and/or school districts when they develop achievement tests. Consequently, achievement tests grade level expectations are often not consistent with state and/or school district grade level expectations. Often, the district's curriculum expectations may be considerably higher or even lower. This contributes to the fact that the achievement test is unable to measure the effects of instruction and is unable to contribute to instructional decision making and planning.

In various research studies, general education teachers and special education teachers have reported that achievement test results are useless when trying to make instructional decisions. They also reported that for that reason, they are left trying to judge instructional effectiveness and student performance using informal observations; however, research has shown that using informal observations for this purpose is problematic. Teachers typically were biased towards judging that students had mastered educational skills beyond what they actually had. Because standardized achievement tests are limited in regards to making instructional decisions, teachers have had to resort to practices which have been shown to be inadequate.

A final criticism of achievement tests has to do with the idea of creating a national norm. Before achievement tests are published, they are administered nationally to a small sample of students to create what is called a *national norm*. Norms are the typical scores that students of various ages typically received on the test. Thus, when the test is administered to a student, his score can be compared to the national norm to see where his performance falls in relation to others of similar age or grade level. On the surface that sounds like a good idea. However, there are a few problems with that process.

First, let's go back to the discussion about curriculum. Curricula vary from state to state and in some cases, school district to school district. Assuming that you can just collect a bunch of scores from across the nation and lump them together to create a national norm is incorrect. Different students from different parts of the country have been exposed to different curricula, and possess academic skills that are specific to where they live. There is not a national curriculum to provide the consistency to develop a meaningful national norm.

Instruction varies from classroom to classroom. Teachers do not teach the same way in every classroom across the nation. Thus to assume that instruction is the same across the country and thus a national norm is appropriate is incorrect. Again, think about it logically. Does it seem appropriate to compare the performance of a student living in inner city Richmond, Virginia, to the performance of a student living in Beverly Hills, California? It is unlikely that those two students were exposed to the same curriculum or the same instruction. National norms may not accurately represent various geographical regions, various races, various cultural backgrounds, and various socio-economic statuses. Considering all of this, many educational professionals and parents conclude that the validity of the use of IQ and achievement tests as a means of identifying students as eligible for special education services is dubious at best. Yet, the discrepancy model continues to be used to make determinations regarding the educational eligibility and placement of students. We will now examine the discrepancy model itself and the issues that have been identified in the research regarding that process.

6
the discrepancy model

When the federal government was first considering including the category of Learning Disabilities in the Individuals with Disabilities in Education Act, they were not sure how students with disabilities should be identified. Because they were of mixed opinions as to how to define the term Learning Disability, they were not sure how they were going to be able to manage the number of students who might be identified as LD. The definition of a learning disability (both then and now) is a definition of exclusions. In other words, if the evaluation determines that the problem is not this and not that, then it may be a learning disability. The first option to deal with the anticipated problem of prevalence was to place a two percent cap on the category of LD, meaning only two percent of a school district's student population could be identified as LD. The two percent idea must not have had much support, because just prior to IDEA's becoming a law, the idea of using a discrepancy model was introduced. At the time, the discrepancy model was just a theory; despite this, it gained support and was determined to be a way to identify students as learning disabled. At face value, it really does seem to make sense. Compare the student's theoretical level of intelligence (IQ) to their level of academic achievement. If they are not performing up to their level of potential, then they must have learning problems, or be learning disabled.

The trouble lies in that it is just a theory, and the research has shown that there are several problems with the theory. The first set of problems has to do with the use of IQ tests, discussed in chapter four. The second set of problems has to do with the use of achievement tests, discussed in chapter five. The final set of problems has to do with the discrepancy model itself.

There are a few different types of discrepancy models, and all of them have been shown in research to have severe limitations. The most often used discrepancy model is the discrepancy between IQ score and achievement score. This model has been repeatedly shown to be incapable of differentiating between students that are actually learning disabled and those students that are just low achieving (slow learners). When a student was identified as having a learning disability, it would be hoped that the decision would be a reliable one. The research has shown that this identification is far from reliable. In fact, the agreement rate has been shown to be between .57 and .86. This means that if a student is evaluated and identified as having a learning disability, and then the student is evaluated again, the second evaluation will again identify the student as having a learning disability only about 57 to 86 percent of the time. Students who are evaluated and identi- fied as not having a learning disability can be reevaluated and identified as having a learning disability about 57 percent of the time. So there is a significant lack of consistency in the decisions that are made using the discrepancy model. But, it gets worse.

What if a student is evaluated and identified as a student with a learning disability, then, the student is evaluated again, but this time different tests are used? Perhaps a different IQ test or a different achievement test is used. The agreement rates between the first and second evaluation drops to .25. This means that if four stu- dents were identified as having a learning disability, and then those four students were evaluated again using different tests, but this time only one of those four students would be found to have a learning disability after the second evaluation. This lack of consistency is alarming and leads to decisions about special education eligibility that seem to be arbitrary. Such lack of reliability can create chaos when a student identified in one district as LD moves ten miles into a neighboring district and is determined (through reevaluation) to no longer qualify for special education. This usually occurs because either different assessment tests were used or because that district's point difference for discrepancy is different from the first district's. The unfortunate result is the same. The student no longer qualifies for special education services, not because his disability has been "fixed" but because the student moved ten miles into another district.

Some researchers have concluded that because of this lack of consistency and apparently arbitrary decision making, the discrepancy model is actually ignored by school staff who make special education eligibility decisions. In 1997 the

Individuals with Disabilities in Education Act was rewritten, and the new included the alternative discrepancy method. This method proposed that if student is evaluated and found to not have the discrepancy needed to identify him or her as a student with a learning disability, then the school staff making the special education eligibility decision could still identify that student as having a learning disability if they believed he really did have one. This led to school districts all over the nation ignoring the discrepancy model. Obviously someone in 1997 knew that the discrepancy model was not working, so why did we not get rid of it then? If you are wondering if the lack of reliability in LD eligibility criteria might somehow lead to a large number of students identified as learning disabled, you would be absolutely correct. Across the United States, in any given school district, slightly higher than 50% of all students identified as being in need of special education are classified as learning disabled.

Another criticism of the discrepancy model, and this has a lot to do with the limitations of achievement tests, is that it is not sensitive to the developmental stages of learning. A good example is reading. Elementary age students and secondary age students may both display significant difficulties with reading; however, the root of these difficulties is likely to be different. Elementary age students likely will struggle with phonological awareness (the understanding of the sounds letters make) and word identification skills. Secondary age students likely will have difficulties with fluency and comprehension. Standardized tests are not sensitive to these differences. Remember, the questions on these achievement tests only assess large chunks of generic curriculum. Additionally, achievement tests do a dismal job of assessing curriculum in the early grades, kindergarten through second grade. Curiously, these are the grades that research has consistently pointed to when discussing the effectiveness of early prevention and intervention. Thus, students in grades kindergarten through second grade are required to do very little on achievement tests to receive a score within the average range, so only about two percent of first graders who have difficulties in phonological awareness and word identification would display the necessary discrepancy to qualify for special education services. However, about 25% of high school students would be identified by the discrepancy model. The discrepancy model leads to an under-identification of younger children, and an over-identification of secondary children. I have actually worked in schools where the principal had made the proclamation that no kindergarten or first grade students were to be evaluated for

eligibility because they never qualified. The principal saw evalu-
~arten and first graders to be a waste of time and resources. It
d why all of this is problematic when you study intervention

Research shows that intervention and prevention is most successful when it occurs early. In education, it is recommended that it should happen before the students turn eight years old in order to maximize the effects. The discrepancy model has been shown to actually prevent early intervention. Research has shown that across the county the average age of a student placed in special education is ten years old. That means that despite knowing that early intervention is most effective (i.e., kindergarten, first, and second grades) the discrepancy model postpones intervention until the student is in the fifth grade. This is much too late, and is why the discrepancy model is commonly referred to as the "Wait to Fail" model. Students often have to fail academically in the early grades until they finally display the discrepancy necessary to qualify as a student with a disability. Again the root of the problem here are the achievement tests.

The content on achievement tests does not adequately assess curriculum from kindergarten, first, and second grade. It is only a slight exaggeration to say that if students in kindergarten, first, or second grade can write their names on the test, they will get a score within the average range. But, they will not display the necessary discrepancy until their academic achievement falls low enough to be discrepant from their IQ. This usually does not happen until the later grades. When they finally qualify for special education services, the effectiveness of the intervention is diminished by its tardiness. Perhaps this is the reason why students who are placed in special education are rarely dismissed from special education.

The traditional method of identifying students as eligible for special education services as a student with a learning disability has depended upon the discrepancy model. This method has also always focused on the student. It is assumed that the problem lies within the student. This is problematic because often students who displayed a discrepancy and were identified as having a learning disability were, in actuality, instructional casualties. Instructional casualties are students who were not exposed to early literacy skills, were given marginally effective instruction, were exposed to instruction that had not been scientifically validated, or were given instruction that was implemented with poor integrity. For these reasons, students exhibit gaps in their educational skills. Then, because of these gaps, they exhibit a discrepancy and are erroneously identified as a student with a learning disability, when in actuality they just need quality instruction/intervention to fill the gaps. This is what is wrong with assuming that the problem lies within the student.

Other factors need to be considered, such as the instructional environment in which the student is asked to learn. Also, the instruction that the student has received in the past and is receiving should be evaluated, along with the curriculum to which the student is exposed. Before assuming that the problem lies within the student, the environment, curriculum, and instruction should be evaluated to ensure that they are appropriate for promoting positive educational outcomes.

Given all of these difficulties with IQ testing, achievement testing, and the discrepancy model, why do we continue to use this method of identifying students as learning disabled? There are several reasons. First, the majority of educators are creatures of habit. The discrepancy model has been in use since 1975 and we are very comfortable with it and resistant to change. Change is uncomfortable. Second, assuming that a problem lies within the child is comforting for teachers. It is much easier to attribute the difficulties to the student than to shoulder the responsibility of adjusting a classroom and/or instruction to meet a student's needs. Who is going to go to a teacher and say that his/her way of teaching is not effective for this student and that he/she needs to change what he/she is doing? That might make for an extremely uncomfortable situation, but perhaps it needs to happen more often for the good of children. Teach children where they are; don't expect them to come to where you are teaching.

Finally, there is big business. Large corporations make money selling tests and test protocols. Corporations that produce IQ tests and achievement tests need to have school staff who continue to purchase those tests and the forms needed for those tests to enable those businesses to continue to make billions of dollars. Despite the research showing that the discrepancy formula is not working, it continues to be included in federal and state laws. Lobbyists for these corporations have the funding to get the ears of politicians to make sure the discrepancy model remains in federal and state laws and regulations.

However, the winds of change are blowing. A small group of knowledgeable educators is beginning to fight the good fight. They are standing up for what is right for children. Finally, the focus is on the children for the right reasons. New ideas have been introduced and they are gaining support. People are starting to see that past practices are not planted in concrete and that change, while difficult, can be brought about. Things can be done differently. What are these new ideas and why are they better for children? Let's begin by examining an approach called Response to Intervention (RTI).

7

what is response to intervention?

A discrepancy formula requires using an evaluation process to identify the student as either eligible or not eligible for special education services. Different states have different regulations as to how much time school staff are allowed to complete this process. Some states say that a special education eligibility decision has to be made within 90 days, some say 75 days, and some say 65 days. The amount of time is not what is critical, what is important is the focus of school staff during this time of consideration. Primarily, the focus of the discrepancy model during this period is on determining whether or not the student has a disability. Can the student be "diagnosed" with something, so that we can put him/her into special education so that he/she can get the "help" that he/she needs?

There are two flaws in that way of thinking. First, there is very little attention paid to what the specific needs of the student are. In fact, the student's needs usually are not considered until the very end, and that is only if the student is found eligible for special education services. This goes back to the scenario described at the beginning of the book. A lot of time is spent trying to find a disorder within the student through testing. If one is found, then at the meeting at the end of the process, someone finally asks what the needs of the student are. Usually the person who asks this question is the special education teacher who is going to be teaching the student, and she is asking so that she can write an education plan to implement with the student in order to help him/her. That's when the school staff encounter the problems with IQ and achievement tests that have been previously discussed.

Because these tests lack specificity, they do not adequately reflect the curriculum of all grade levels, and because they are not sensitive to the effects of instruction, they are of limited helpfulness when trying to make instructional decisions and planning instruction. Thus, special education teachers are given very little information on which to base the education plan for that student. Research and experience have shown that most special education teachers then employ a laundry list of things that the student will need to work on. Too often this allows for the creation of an education plan that is not specific to the student's unique educational needs. This leads to another question: What's so *special* about special education?

Spending all that time looking for a disorder within the child causes a second problem. It encourages the mindset that "help" is special education, and that special education is a *place* instead of a continuum of graduated support services. It also facilitates the mindset that the only way that a student can receive "help" is to "go to" special education. This is why general education teachers refer students and want them tested immediately to see if they qualify. The truth is that help can come in many shapes and forms, and can come without special education. In fact, help should come without special education whenever possible. It is always better to provide the assistance a student needs within the general education setting and not identify a child as a special education student whenever possible. Labels are meant for jelly jars, not for children.

So what if we reversed the process and reversed the traditional way of thinking? What if we spent the 90 days, 75 days (or however many days a particular state allows) identifying the student's needs and attempting to meet those needs? The staff could worry about whether the student had a disability at the end of the process. This is sometimes referred to as reversal of the eligibility-need continuum. This would encourage educators to address specific student needs in the general education setting first. Then, if the student still was not successful, educators would know that he was in need of special education. Essentially, it would be a process of matching the intensity of services to the intensity of the student's needs. It becomes a sequential process when the intensity of the services is stepped up until the student becomes successful. Keep in mind that these services are interventions provided in the general education setting. The highest intensity of service would be special education services, but the student only receives those services when it is demonstrated with data that this is the level of service that he/she needs to be successful. When that evidence is documented, then the student is provided with those services. There are no labels necessary. Students are just

identified as entitled to the highest intensity of service. There is no need to identify (or label) the student as Learning Disabled, Mentally Disabled, etc.

To implement such a system, educators will need some tools. The two things that
they will need are: Curriculum-Based Evaluation and a Problem-Solving Model.
When these two are combined, they create a process called Response to Intervention (RTI). Let's explore the details and benefits of these tools, and then we will
discuss implementation of a Response to Intervention model in more detail.

6

curriculum-based evaluation

You may not have not heard of Curriculum-Based Evaluation (CBE), but it has been around for a long time. Sometimes you will see it referred to as Curriculum-Based Measurement or perhaps Curriculum-Based Assessment, but they are all basically the same thing. CBM are assessment tools that are created by teachers and are derived directly from the student's actual classroom curriculum. CBA is the same thing as CBM except it is not created by a teacher; it is selected from an existing set of assessments or a program. CBE are assessment tools derived from the curriculum created by a teacher (or selected from an existing package) and used in conjunction with a problem-solving model.

CBE are very short tests – usually one minute long – that assess specific academic skills. For example in the area of reading, you would have CBE assessments for letter identification, phoneme (letter sounds) identification, blend (two letter sounds) identification, sight word identification, identifying words in sentences, identifying words in passages, etc. Remember, one of the criticisms of achievement tests was that they lacked specificity and because of that, they were not useful when making decisions on what to teach students. CBE possesses the necessary specificity, and they can be administered in a short period of time. Reading and math CBE assessments have a one-minute administration time, while written expression has a three-minute administration time. So, they have a much shorter administration time, and they provide better data. CBE also allows educators to specifically identify a student's strengths and weaknesses within broad skills. Using the above example of reading, if we administer all of those CBE assessments with a student, we would be able to identify the student's specific strengths and weaknesses within reading. Then we would know in what specific skill areas the student needed instruction/intervention to strengthen his weaknesses.

The following is an example of a CBE probe for nonsense words taken from the Basic Skill Builders set:

										Correct	Error
									First Try		
									Second Try		

SEE TO SAY

Blending Sounds with Both Long and Short Vowels

Directions: Say each sound.

shud	nane	flib	cate	phude	claf	chet	brin	phode	(9)
whote	plime	blox	twile	brug	theme	rollo	clak	drask	(18)
glape	snat	crend	tompt	blep	rosk	kine	quip	bode	(27)
frodo	ship	sito	stos	chike	slone	base	tite	pove	(36)
mump	tast	thrud	flisp	stete	shape	splam	lipe	frew	(45)
shas	dife	phob	cuse	brik	spile	clift	nint	wile	(54)
theck	grun	pleb	quit	zone	frust	goke	phig	glid	(63)
dasp	cril	fruf	stut	snim	whave	thas	chez	mote	(72)
spip	rime	thit	frak	dresk	phono	crump	pano	whes	(81)
glish	dral	bine	vamp	chip	tune	slap	tefe	snop	(90)
phat	fluft	crend	presk	blosp	thap	whipe	glape	spift	(99)
blox	slimp	vepe	bufe	quile	rame	blep	chasp	blox	(108)

Basic Skill Builders   BSB-1

But what happens after that? So we identify the student's specific strengths and weaknesses, and we teach the student according to his weaknesses, but how do we know if what we are doing is being effective? Well, in the traditional model we would not know. In the traditional model interventions would have been recommended, and then sometime later someone would have asked the teacher if it was effective. Experience has taught us that usually the teacher is not sure, at best. So, one is left guessing about the intervention effectiveness. The inherent problem in such a pre-referral approach is simply that such an approach is easily turned into a "rubber stamp" procedure used to expedite the student's entrance into testing for special education eligibility determination. There must be a better way, right?

CBE allows educators to collect data to make data-based decisions regarding the effectiveness of the instruction. Since the CBE assessments take little time to give, they can be administered frequently – even on a daily basis if needed – to allow for monitoring of the student's progress as a result of the instruction. So while the educator is teaching a skill to a student, the student's progress can be assessed to determine if the student is learning the skill. If the student fails to show progress, then the educator knows that the method of instruction is not working and something different needs to be done with that student. In other words, this approach corrects itself. You do not have to wait several weeks or months to determine that the student is not making adequate academic progress and is in danger of failing. Therefore this approach can be characterized as "self-correcting". Since CBE can be administered on a daily basis, the decisions regarding the effectiveness can be made weekly. This eliminates several problems: not knowing whether or not the student is learning as a result of instruction, ineffective instructional techniques by teachers for long periods of time, and the "Wait to Fail" process.

Research has demonstrated that CBE can be used this way. A study was conducted over a ten-week period using both CBE and achievement tests to assess student progress as a result of instruction showed that the CBE results indicated that the student was learning as a result of the instruction, while the achievement test results showed that the student was making no progress. CBE was sensitive to the small increases in the student's academic skills, where the achievement tests were not. The use of CBE has also been shown to increase student achievement whether the student is identified as a general education student, a student with a learning disability, or a student receiving academic assistance. This is especially true if the results are charted with the student. Because CBE is measured using whole numbers (raw scores), it is very easy to understand. Achievement tests use standard scores, percentile ranks, age equivalent scores, and grade equivalent scores. These can be very hard to understand, even for educators. CBE uses whole numbers, which improves communication between educators and between educators and parents. You can easily understand that your child is identifying 21 phonemes correctly in a minute, and he should be identifying 43 phonemes correctly in a minute. It is much easier to understand, plus the results can be charted to create a visual image of the student's skill acquisition. A student's baseline level of performance, or performance before instruction/intervention, can be charted. Then the goal level of performance expected for that student can be charted. By connecting the baseline to the goal, it creates an aim line. This aim line is the progress that an educator expects to see as a result of the instruction/intervention. So, the progress monitoring data can then be charted during the intervention to see if the progress the student is making follows the aim line. If it is, then the educator knows that the student is learning as a result of the instruction. If it is not, then the educator knows that the instruction needs to be changed to meet the student's needs.

Using the example above and looking at the chart below; Tim's (the student) baseline of 21 phonemes is charted, and then his goal of 43 phonemes is charted. Connecting these two points established an aim line for Tim's progress. The progress monitoring data would be charted and compared to the aim line. The consecutive yellow dots above the aim line would indicate that the student is making the expected progress, and that the instruction being used with the student is effective. The three consecutive yellow dots below the aim line indicate a lack of progress and a need for a change in the instruction being used with the student.

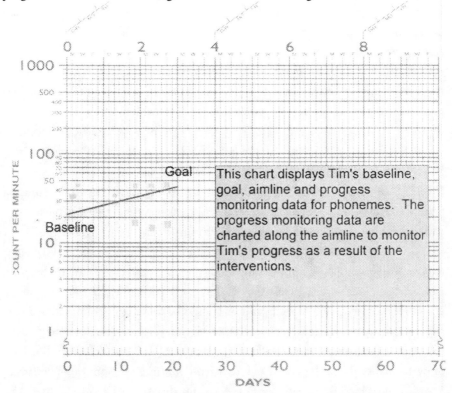

This chart displays Tim's baseline, goal, aimline and progress monitoring data for phonemes. The progress monitoring data are charted along the aimline to monitor Tim's progress as a result of the interventions.

This becomes even more powerful when the student is taught to chart his own progress monitoring data. The student then begins to see his progress and begins to "buy into" his educational progress. The student will want to start beating his previous scores and get better and better, work harder and harder, and learn more and more. The power lies in the student's wanting to improve his academic skills and wanting to see his or her progress monitoring data points go up the chart.

They not only start to progress academically, but they also start to feel better about themselves. Competition is not with others, but with ones own performance.

A final advantage to CBE is that it allows for peer referencing. Remember, one of the criticisms of achievement tests is that they are nationally normed by being given to students all over the county to create norms. So when they are administered to your child, how your child performs compared to students all over the nation determines his/her score. There are several problems with that (as previously discussed). That process assumes that your child is similar to the other children culturally, ethnically, and lives in similar geographic region. Additionally, it assumes that every student in the nation is exposed to similar instruction, a similar instructional environment, and to similar curricula. Wouldn't it make more sense to compare your child's score to students who live in the same geographic region, are similar racially and ethnically, and have been exposed to the same instruction, instructional environment, and curriculum?

Since CBE have short administration time, educators can administer them to a sample of students in the school district in which your child learns. That allows for the creation of norms from students living in your school district, all of whom have been exposed to similar instruction, and have been taught from the same curriculum. Thus, your child's performance is compared to his actual peers. When you think about it, why would you do it any other way? It just makes sense, and the research has shown that is decreases bias in special education eligibility decisions. In fact by using this exact process, one school district was found to decrease the number of black males placed in special education by 45% in the first year of implementation! In the second year of implementation, they decreased the number of black males placed in special education by another 28%!

The inherent strength of CBE is that it is derived directly from the classroom curriculum that is used to teach the student. Curricula are different from state to state and are taught differently from school to school, so it is important that we assess students based on what they are being taught. Achievement tests do not adjust to assess what a student is expected to know. They are the exact same for every student, so what is assessed on an achievement test and what the student has been taught do not correlate. Educators need instruction-based assessments like CBE to provide them with all of the benefits and to provide students with the instruction/intervention that they deserve.

9
a problem-solving model

The benefits of curriculum-based assessment tools are maximized when they are implemented within an operational framework. That framework is provided by a problem solving model. The number of students placed in special education services from 1977 to 1994 grew from 3.7 million to 5.3 million, despite school enrollment remaining constant. Collaborative problem solving by a school-based team is believed to be a way to eliminate the number of students being considered for special education eligibility who do not need to be considered and to increase the legitimacy of those students that are considered for special education eligibility. A problem-solving model has seven basic steps, and they are as follows:

- Define the Problem.

- Develop an Assessment Plan.

- Implement the Assessment Plan.

- Analyze the Results of the Assessment Plan.

- Develop an Intervention Plan.

- Implement the Intervention Plan.

- Analyze the Results of the Intervention Plan.

This model is very similar to the scientific method in the chart below:

Scientific Method vs Problem Solving Model

Scientific Method

- Observe or identify a problem or phenomenon-generate hypothesis.
- Test the hypothesis by an assessment-generate data.
- Draw conclusions and integrate results into the existing body of knowledge.
- Progress monitor under same environment circumstances or replicate under different circumstances.

Problem-Solving Steps

- Define problem (What is the problem?)
- Develop an assessment plan.
- Analysis of assessment plan (Why does the problem exist?)
- Development of intervention (What should be done to address the problem?)
- Analysis of intervention plan (Did the intervention work?)
- Progress monitor.

This process occurs at four different levels, as seen in the graphic below. The purpose of this process is to match the intensity of services to the intensity of the student's needs. The intensity of the services (or interventions) is increased until the level of services are identified that are necessary for the student to be success-ful.

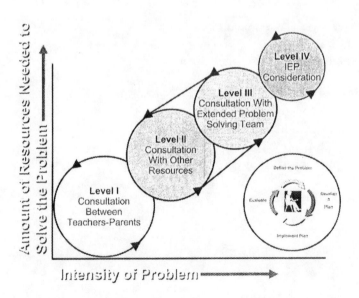

The first three levels all call for implementation in the general education setting, with levels one and two requiring informal implementation and level three requiring formal implementation. Because the first three levels are implemented in the general education setting, it is imperative that general education staff believe in the process. Implementation of this type of model should not be viewed as a special education initiative; it should be viewed as an educational initiative. However, the entire burden of implementation cannot be placed on general education. Special education staff should act as resource persons and consultants to their general education counterparts. The lines that have been drawn (and in some circumstances the barriers that have been built) separating general education from special education must come down. This model calls for shared accountability for all children by all school staff. This is consistent with the No Child Left Behind legislation.

The fourth level calls for formal implementation within the special education setting. Keep in mind that the purpose of the process is to match the intensity of the services to the intensity of the student's needs. So if the student's needs are not met in level one, then the educator moves on to level two. If the student's needs are not met in level two, then the educator moves on to level three. Then if the student's needs are not met after implementation at level three, the student is considered for eligibility for level four, which is special education services.

When a student is having difficulty, either academic or behavioral, **level one** requires the teacher contact the parents and have a meeting. This is a major difference from the traditional process when the parents were contacted when the school needed permission to test the student and had typically not been involved in the process until then. At level one the teacher and the parents work through the problem-solving process on an informal basis.

The teacher and parents should spend some time discussing the problem and generating some hypotheses as to why they think the problem is occurring. They can then collaboratively analyze data that the teacher has on the student. The data at this point usually are work samples, teacher observations, previous test results, etc. In schools where CME is being implemented schoolwide, the teacher should have CBE data to evidence the needs of the student. If they decide at the meeting that more information is needed to understand the problem, then they create a data collection plan and they implement that plan. After reviewing baseline data, the teacher and parents should brainstorm intervention ideas based upon the data that they have. In this process, every decision is made based on data. All guess-work is eliminated. This is a data-based decision making process.

Following the generation of intervention ideas, the length of time for the inter-ventions to be implemented is decided and a method of progress monitoring is decided upon. Again, this is informal implementation so CBE does not have to be used to progress monitor at this point. Rather, work samples can be collected or teacher observations can be used to determine the effectiveness of the interven-tions. Of course, the best practice would be that the teacher employs CBE prac-tices in the classroom. The progress of the students in the class can be monitored daily using CBE. Students who exhibit a need for re-teaching of concepts can be identified quickly.

It is important that assessment, progress monitoring, and adjustment of instruc-tion based on progress monitoring results be considered just as important as in-struction itself. Following the intervention phase, the teacher and parents would meet again to discuss the effectiveness of the interventions.

Again, the data collected allows for determination of the student's progress. Based on the data collected that monitors progress, the decision is made as to whether or not the process can be stopped at this point, or whether the student needs to move on to level two.

At **level two** the Problem Solving Model (PSM) cycle begins again, but the dif-ference from level one is that more people are involved. Bringing in more people allows for the problem to be analyzed by people with different perspectives, dif-ferent skills, and different levels of experience. Some schools choose to complete level two implementation by having grade level teams meet with the parent and discuss the student's difficulties. So if the student is a first grade student, then the teacher and the parents would meet with all of the first grade teachers. The student's difficulties would be discussed, along with presentation of some base-line data. Work samples are reviewed and each teacher hypothesizes as to why he/she thinks the problem may be occurring. If more data are needed to better understand the problem, then an assessment plan is developed for the teacher to implement with the student.

Once all of the necessary data are collected, the team meets again to review the data and develop an intervention plan. The different teachers bring different experiences to the meeting. Some may have had a student with similar difficulties before and know what was successful with that previous student. Some may have a thorough knowledge of interventions in the student's area of difficulty and can share that knowledge. At level two, some schools also choose to involve support personnel such as the school psychologist, the school counselor, the reading specialist, speech therapist, or the assistant principal. These people have different educational backgrounds and experiences and can provide different perspectives and intervention ideas.

Once an intervention plan is developed, then the plan is implemented and the teacher monitors the student's progress to examine the effects of the interventions. At the conclusion of the intervention phase, the progress monitoring data are reviewed to decide the next step. School staff need to allow the data to make the decision for them. Did the student display progress based on the progress monitoring data? Best practice would be for CBE to be used here for progress monitoring, but because this is still informal implementation, work samples and teacher observations can be used. If the student still does not evidence the expected, the student's case can be referred on to **level three** for formal implementation to begin.

10
level three -
formal implementation

It is important at this point to define interventions. In an RTI model Interventions have two components: progress monitoring and explicit instruction. Progress monitoring simply means that while the intervention is being implemented, data are collected to determine the effects of the intervention. This is a data-based decision-making process and therefore data must be collected. At levels one and two, progress monitoring data can simply be work samples and teacher observations. However, best practice would be for CBE to be used. In level three, CBE is required for progress monitoring.

Progress monitoring occurs by establishing a baseline of the student's performance prior to intervention. Then a goal must be established that the teacher and parent would like to see the student achieve as a result of the intervention. This is done informally at levels one and two; however, in level three this is completed formally, which will be discussed later. Thus, while intervening, the progress monitoring data that are collected informs educators as to whether the student is progressing towards the stated goal. At the end of levels one and two the data-based decision is: does the student's progress monitoring data indicate that he made progress towards the established goal, and did he meet the established goal?

The second component of an intervention is explicit instruction. A trained school staff member must sit down and teach the student. Far too often, classroom intervention plans are comprised of non-teaching interventions such as preferential seating, modified assignments, praise and attention, and/or a peer tutor. None of these involve the school's staff teaching the student in his specific area of weakness – thus none of them are interventions. They are technically accommodations and modifications, but not interventions. How can we expect a student to make progress if nothing is being done with the student to strengthen his/her areas of weakness? We must strengthen his area of weakness by teaching skills that he/she lacks. This may seem like common sense, but believe me, I have traveled from state to state and seen "intervention plans" that comprise of nothing more than preferential seating, modified assignments, praise and attention, and peer tutoring.

Level three calls for implementation of the PSM in a more formal format using a collaborative team process. This is typically accomplished using the assistance team or student study team format using completion of PSM forms and implementation of CBE procedures as key components. Assistance teams or student study teams are school based teams comprised of several school staff members. This usually includes a general education representative, a special education representative, a speech therapist, a school psychologist, a school counselor, a reading specialist, and an administrator. At times the school nurse and curriculum specialist may also be asked to participate.

When defining the problem, the team is charged with the task of generating hypotheses as to why the problem is occurring. Hypotheses are typically brainstormed in four areas: Environment, Curriculum, Instruction, and the Learner. The Learner is always considered last, because one of the basic tenants of this process is that you must ensure that the environment, curriculum, and the instruction are appropriate for the learner to learn, **before** you can assume that the root of the problem lies within the learner.

Once hypotheses are generated, the team develops an assessment plan that will allow them to collect data to determine which hypotheses are supported and which are refuted. Multi-dimensional assessment procedures are implemented following the RIOT mnemonic which stands for Review, Interview, Observe, and Test. Each of these assessment procedures is considered for each of the four domains, Environment, Curriculum, Instruction, and Learner. The testing utilized here can involve standardized procedures, but typically involves CBE techniques. The team completes forms to define the problem and develops an assessment plan. These two tasks are usually completed with the parents at the first meeting.

No decisions are made in an RTI model without using data. This is why no interventions are proposed until the data from the assessment plan have been collected.

Only then can data-based decisions be made concerning the specific strengths and weaknesses of the student. This allows for research-based prescriptive interventions to be implemented which address the specific needs of the student. In short, it eliminates the guesswork inherent in traditional approaches. Without using baseline data to determine interventions, assistance teams tend to guess at what they think the student's problem is and then try an intervention that they think might work. Or, they might plug in the same intervention every time, regardless of the problem the student is having.

The data collected from the assessment plan serves as the student's baseline, and goals are set that the team would like to see the student achieve as a result of the intervention plan. The assistance team or student study team reconvenes when the assessment plan is completed. The team, along with parental input, must then complete two main tasks. First, the assessment plan data must be analyzed. Second, a data-based intervention plan must be developed. The analysis allows for the identification of the student's specific strengths and weaknesses within the areas of concern. Baseline performances of the specific weaknesses are documented and goals are set for the student.

There are several ways to establish goals. First, a local norming project can be completed across the school district. In the project CBE assessment procedures are conducted with a random sample of students in each grade level across the school district. This allows for obtaining typical scores for academic skill levels for each grade level. For example, a CBE assessment probe for sight words could be completed with a random sample of third graders from across the district. This would tell school district personnel what the typical score is on this probe for third graders. Then if the student going through the assistance team PSM process is a third grader and is having difficulty with sight words, his/her score on the same probe can be compared to the typical score from that school district.

These typical scores are called norms, and in a norming project norms for several academic skills are collected for several grades for the fall, winter and spring. Depending on when the student goes through the assistance team process determines which norm is used. Thus, the norm can serve as the goal for the student once the student's baseline, level of performance prior to intervention, is obtained. So in essence, the goal would be to get the student's level of performance to be commensurate with his/her same grade peers in the school district. It is also possible, through a norming project, to establish the level of performance that represents the possible need for special education services. Thus, if the student's baseline falls below that special education cutoff score, then the goal could be to get the student's level of performance above the special education range. Then the follow-up goal could be to get the student's level of functioning to be commensurate with the local norm.

An additional means of establishing goals is to consider the student's rate of learning. Essentially this means how fast students learn. Again this can be obtained through a local norming project. For example, if a fall local norming project tells you that first grade students can identify 20 sight words correctly in a minute, and a winter local norming project tells you that first graders can identify 40 sight words correctly in a minute, then you can subtract the two to get a difference of 20 sight words. Then, you can divide the 20 sight words by the number of weeks between the fall and winter norming projects, which is usually ten. Dividing 20 by ten establishes the first graders' rate of learning, or more simply it tells you that they learn 2 sight words per week. So, if a first grade student going through the assistance team PSM process has a baseline of 15 sight words and you want to intervene with that student for six weeks, then you know if his rate of learning is commensurate with other first graders in the district then he should learn 12 sight words during that intervention phase. That would mean that his goal should be 15 plus 12 or 27 sight words. This is not to say that these are the only ways of setting goals, but they are three of the best ways. (The benefits of using local norms were discussed in chapter eight, discussing peer referencing.)

PSM forms are used to document that the team completed the Analysis of the Assessment Plan and then the Develop the Intervention Plan steps. Once the data collected from the assessment plan are analyzed, goals are set, and interventions are determined, interventions relevant to the student's specific weaknesses can be identified, and a progress monitoring plan can be established. Progress monitoring data are collected during the intervention phase so that data-based decisions can be made on the effectiveness of the interventions. When the data show that the intervention is not resulting in student progress, then the intervention is changed. Remember CBE can be administered daily, so the effectiveness of an intervention can be evaluated in just a few days. When the data show that a student is not making progress as a result of an intervention, why would school staff continue implementing the intervention? Adjusting interventions and/or increasing intensity of interventions until the student is successful is the nature of the process. Thus, if the data show that the intervention in place is not working, they would stop the intervention and change what is being done with the student. In the PSM model you do not have to wait for a student to fail before you make changes to help the student. Once a progress monitoring plan is determined, then that is the end of the second meeting. So school staff and parents leave the second meeting with a prescriptive research-based intervention plan in place for the student. This idea of prescriptive research based interventions in the PSM is exactly what is called for in No Child Left Behind.

Following implementation of the intervention plan, the team reconvenes with the parent. The purpose of this third meeting is to analyze the progress monitoring data and determine the effectiveness of the intervention plan. The progress monitoring data are reviewed and compared to the pre-established goal to determine the student's response to intervention. A determination is then made as to whether the student made progress and the intervention plan needs to continue; whether a new intervention plan needs to be developed; or whether the student is in need of the highest intensity of service, level four, which is special education. This decision is made based on a convergence of data, and the student must meet established RTI special education eligibility guidelines in order to receive the highest intensity of services.

If it is determined that the student is in need of the highest intensity of services, then the progress monitoring data become the baseline data for level four and the PSM process begins again at level four. Keep in mind that if a student is identified as not responding to the intervention and needing special education services, the progress monitoring data collected throughout the intervention phase documents that, despite the interventions, the student still had significant difficulties. This means that during the intervention phase, the interventions put into place were not effective and were adjusted several times to increase the intensity of the intervention in an attempt to meet the student's need. This is best practice. Concluding that interventions were not successful with a student, and identifying that student as in need of special education services following implementation of just one or two interventions is **not** best practice.

Earlier in this chapter we noted hat implementation of a PSM model is believed to *decrease* the number of students in need of consideration for special education services and *increase* the legitimacy of those students considered for special education services. Research results and implementation experience prove these points. With implementation of the PSM, two elementary schools in Virginia found that 42% of the students who went through the PSM model exhibited performance consistent with their same grade peers at the end of the level three. Students were found to make significant progress regardless of gender, grade, socio-economic status, or race. This has a profound impact on the overrepresentation of minority students in special education services. Additionally, the general education teachers involved in that study reported that they believed that the PSM process benefited students, was effective, provided data that were helpful and good indicators of student performance, and provided helpful interventions for the students.

Another study in South Carolina found that prior to implementing this model 77% of the students that went through the traditional assistance team process went on for special education eligibility consideration, and only 35% of them actually qualified for special education services. In the first year of implementation of the PSM model only 50% of the students that went through the PSM process were considered for special education eligibility, and 75% of them qualified for special education services. Parent satisfaction surveys from that South Carolina school district indicated that they had a higher level of approval for the PSM process than the traditional process. Finally, after one year of implementation, the same school district in South Carolina reported an eight-to-one reduction in the number of students placed in special education services with PSM. In the second year of implementation they reduced the number of students placed in special education services by another six percent. More students were having their needs met in the general education setting through intervention plans, and fewer students needed special education services.

There is also the issue of early intervention and prevention to consider. One of the weaknesses of the discrepancy model is that the use of standardized achievement testing leads to the under-identification of students in kindergarten through second grade as eligible for special education services and over-identification of students in the later grades. (See chapter 6.) This is completely contrary to research that shows that in order to maximize the effectiveness of prevention and intervention, school staff need to intervene prior to age eight.

One particular school district found that implementation of a district-wide RTI model was the answer to this problem. In the first year of RTI implementation they found that 70% of their initial special education placements came from kindergarten through second grade. In the second year of implementation, 76% of their initial placements in special education services came from kindergarten through second grade, while in the third year of implementation, 80% of the initial placements in special education services came from kindergarten through second grade. RTI allowed that school district to intervene early and prevent problems from becoming worse with time. This allowed school staff to provide students with the services that they needed early, resolve the problem, and get students out of special education when they are ready to be successful in regular education. This is completely contrary to the discrepancy model or the "Wait to Fail" model. However, it is exactly what the research says should be done, it is best practice, and it is what students need to be successful.

Tim

There is a more detailed case study provided in the last chapter, but here is an example of how implementation at level three might happen. Tim was a first grade student whom I worked with a few years ago. He was referred to his school's Teacher Assistance Team by his classroom teacher because he was having difficulties with reading. Tim's case had already gone through levels one and two, and the problem was not resolved. So his case was sent to level three, and the Teacher Assistance Team oversaw implementation at the third level. The team started with the task of defining the problem and reviewed background data to find that Tim did not pass a basic reading skills screening given to him at the beginning of first grade. He was receiving help from the speech pathologist because he had some difficulties with articulation of certain sounds. The team hypothesized that Tim was lacking some basic reading skills that prohibited him from reading fluently and comprehending what he read.

Learning to read is like building a pyramid. You have to get those basic building blocks in place before you start to put the more complex skill blocks on top. For reading, the foundation building blocks are skills like being able to identify letters, being able to identify the sounds that letters make (phonemes), being able to identify the sounds that groups of letters make, and being able to identify whole words quickly.

In Tim's case, the team hypothesized that he was weak in one or more of these skills, thus preventing the more complex skills, reading fluently and understanding what is read, from happening. So they developed an assessment plan that proposed using CBE assessments to obtain measures of Tim's letter recognition skills, phoneme identification skills, sound blend identification skills (the sounds that groups of letters make), and sight words.

The team took about one week to complete the assessment plan. The results of the CBE assessments were then analyzed by the team in the Analysis of the Assessment Plan step. The results collected were compared to the school districts norms. Tim was able to identify 21 phonemes correctly per minute. The district norm for his grade level for that time of year was 43 phonemes per minute. This means that while Tim could identify 21 correct letter sounds in a minute, the typical performance for students in his grade level in that school district for that time of year was 43 correct letter sounds. Thus, he was performing significantly below where he should have been. This was also found to be true for sound blends. He was unable to identify any blends correctly, while the norm for his grade level was eight blends in a minute. Tim was able to identify one sight word correctly in a minute, while the norm was 47. His letter identification skills were consistent with the local norm. The data told the team that they needed to intervene with Tim in the areas of phonemes, blends, and sight words. His letter identification skills were not in need of intervention. All of the data collected thus far acted as Tim's baseline data.

The team then developed an intervention plan for the areas that were identified as significant areas of weakness. Remember that in an RTI model, interventions need to have an explicit instruction component. In other words, a trained staff member was going to teach Tim in his areas of difficulty, while monitoring his progress as a result of the instruction. The progress monitoring allowed the team to make short-term, data-based decisions on the effectiveness of the intervention. Tim's baseline data were plotted on a chart. The team chose goals for Tim and those data were plotted. They connected those two points to create an aim line. (An example of this was provided on page 35.)

This is done so that progress monitoring data can be plotted on the chart. The team knew that if the progress monitoring data followed the aim line, then Tim would be making the progress that they expected to see as a result of the intervention. They also knew that if the progress monitoring data fell below the aim line, then the interventions were not working and Tim was not making the progress that they wanted him to make. If that happened, then the team would have to adjust the interventions in an attempt to increase their effectiveness with Tim.

In Tim's case the progress monitoring data indicated that the interventions were extremely effective. Following implementation of the intervention plan, the team completed the Analysis of the Intervention Plan step. In three weeks' time, Tim progressed from 21 phonemes per minute to 46 phonemes per minute. He had also progressed from one sight word per minute to 18 sight words per minute. The teacher reported that Tim's reading fluency and self-confidence were both increasing as a result of the strengthening of his basic reading skills. Through the RTI process, Tim's educational needs were met in the general education setting, and he was never considered for special education eligibility.

11
the highest level of intensity

Level four of the PSM is the only level that involves special education services. It is called the highest level of intensity of intervention. When the student fails to make sufficient progress as a result of level three interventions, then the student is considered for level four eligibility. Level four eligibility is dependent on the following criteria:

- Does the student demonstrate a significantly low level of performance in relations to his peers?

- Does the student display slow growth rates in relation to his peers despite interventions?

- Are number one and number two causing an adverse impact on the student's educational performance?

- Does the student show evidence of a documented need for the highest intensity of intervention?

If the answers to all of these questions are yes, the student can be considered for level four. There is, however, an important component to level four eligibility in the RTI model that is not present in the traditional model. Prior to identifying a student as eligible for level four in an RTI model, the student's exit criteria must be determined. This means that prior to putting a student in special education services, the level of performance that the student must display to exit from level four must be determined. Why is this important? Because nationally the majority of students who go into special education services never progress far enough to come out of those services. In fact, most usually stay in special education until they graduate or drop out of school.

Special education services should be a self-defeating process. Their services should increase student learning to the point that the student no longer needs the special education. This has always been the basic premise of special education, but it rarely happens that way. Think about it this way. What if you went to the doctor, and he told you that he knew what was wrong with you, and he was going to provide medical intervention to remedy the problem. So he provides intervention for a year, but the problem still remains. Then he provides intervention for another year, but the problem still remains. This process continues on for years and years. You continue to receive medical intervention, but you continue to be sick. Would you be happy with those services? Would you not seek a second opinion? Would you not go to another doctor? Then why do we continue to accept our students' receiving special education services, but the problems are never resolved and the students never exit the program?

The answer to this dilemma lies in the RTI model. Traditionally, special education services have been provided, and the student's progress as a result of these services was never assessed – or it was assessed inappropriately. The problem lies in using standardized achievement test results in an attempt to measure progress as a result of instruction. It simply cannot be done. The bigger problem is basing IEPs on achievement test data. An IEP is an Individualized Education Plan. Every student who receives special education services has an IEP. It is the plan that will be used to instruct the student. However, research and implementation experience has taught us that achievement tests provide poor measures of student skills, cannot measure progress as a result of instruction, and cannot be used to make instructional decisions. So essentially IEPs are written and left until a year later when it is time to write another one. Additionally, the student's progress as a result of instruction is never assessed, and instruction is never adjusted. So, it is assumed that the instruction the student is receiving is being effective and the student is making progress.

By implementing the RTI model at level four, a student's IEP is of much higher quality. The progress monitoring data that were collected at the end of level three are used as the baseline data of the IEP. Remember that this baseline data are curriculum-based assessment data, thus the assessment is of specific academic skills. This allows for special education instruction to be provided to the student that is more specific to the student's academic needs. Again, curriculum-based assessments can be used on a daily basis to monitor the student's progress as a result of instruction. If the student is not making progress, the data show that, and the special education teacher can change the instruction being used with the student. Why continue to use ineffective instruction? Continuing to use ineffective instruction is one of the reasons students rarely come out of special education services.

In an RTI model, the student's exit criteria are decided prior to providing level four services. That exit criteria is established as the long-term goal and progress monitoring data are collected while the student receives the highest intensity of intervention. If the student is not progressing towards that exit criteria as a result of the instruction, then the instruction is changed to meet the student's needs. Changes are then routinely made to bring about student progress, to increase the student's level of academic performance, and to get the student out of special education. _*That*_ **would make special education special!**

Does the research support this line of thinking? In a study of fifty special education teachers, 90% of this group of teachers reported that using curriculum-based assessment data improved IEP goal development, student progress monitoring, and instructional decision making. In another study with 14 special education teachers working towards their Master's Degrees, all 14 stated that CBM-type data were more closely connected to curriculum, more connected to instructional strategies, allowed for improved IEP goals, and allowed for more accurate progress monitoring. Those teachers reported that using CBM-type data for the basis of an individualized education plan allowed for the development of a higher quality individualized education plan (IEP).

12
response to intervention and standards-based testing

Research and implementation experience has taught some schools that the line of reasoning in an RTI model works for all students. Some have chosen to implement an RTI model that uses three levels instead of four. This three level process allows for implementation with all students in the school. In the first level, all students in the school are screened using curriculum-based assessments. This allows for the identification of students who are at-risk and will be in need of some type of intervention in order to be successful. Keep in mind that this screening takes place in the fall, so baselines for various academic skills are collected at the beginning of the school year. This informs the school staff as to which students are at risk for struggling throughout the school year. It tells them which students will need additional exposure to concepts to increase their understanding. It also tells them which students are going to need more intense interventions to be successful throughout the school year.

The matching of appropriate interventions to the students' needs then occurs in level two, similar to the levels two and three in the four-level model. If the students display a lack of response to intervention, then they are considered for special education services, which is level three in the level three model. The problem-solving process is the same in the three level model as it is in the four level model. Curriculum-based type assessments are used in both models, also.

An outgrowth of the three level model is to apply the idea of setting a goal for all students in the school. This is similar to the idea of exit criteria previously discussed, but it is applied to **all** students in the school. Baselines are collected for all students in the fall, goals are set, and the progress monitoring is done with all students throughout the school year to determine if they are making progress towards the set goals. If they are not making progress towards the goals, then instruction is adjusted to increase student progress. The next question is: what is used to set the goals?

As a result of the No Child Left Behind law, states have begun developing state curriculum standards and requiring schools to administer state-developed tests to assess student performance in those curriculum standards. Every spring schools administer these tests to students to determine how the students are performing in relation to the standards that the state has developed. There is an abundance of research that shows that curriculum-based assessments in reading fluency (how fluidly the student reads) have a high correlation with passing scores on the standards-based tests. In other words, how well students do on CBM reading fluency measures accurately predicts whether they will pass standards-based language arts tests. This research has even gone as far as to identify how many words students need to be able to read per minute from grades first through sixth in order to significantly increase their likelihood of passing the standards based language arts tests.

What if these reading fluency scores were used as the goal for each student depending on the grade level? The reading fluency for every student in the school could be screened in the fall. That allows the school to match interventions to student needs, based on that baseline reading fluency score. Then the goal is the grade level appropriate reading fluency score needed in order to significantly increase the likelihood of achieving a passing score on the standards-based language arts test. The school then progress monitors with each student throughout the school year and adjusts instruction as needed to move the student's reading fluency score towards the set goal. Thus, prior to taking the standards based language arts test in the spring, the school already knows with a high level of accuracy if the student is going to obtain a passing score. The reading fluency scores can be found in the chart below. Keep in mind these reading fluency scores only predict passing scores on the language arts standards-based test. Math fluency scores have also been identified, however.

- **Fluency benchmarks set by research (Deno)**

  - ❏ 1st grade – 60 wpm

  - ❏ 2nd grade – 90 wpm

  - ❏ 3rd grade – 120 wpm

  - ❏ 4th grade – 130 wpm

  - ❏ 5th grade – 140 wpm

  - ❏ 6th grade – 150 wpm

This process allows for educators to make data based instructional decisions for all students. This idea has been given lip service in the past, but the data used previously have been inappropriate. Curriculum-based assessment data allow for this process to happen for every student. Student progress can be assessed continually, and instruction that is ineffective can be changed. The Problem Solving Model (PSM) is the framework that allows all of this to happen. Recent research of a three-level RTI model has shown that not only does it benefit students, but it also generates increased student performance district wide.

Burns, Appleton, and Stehouwer analyzed the effects of a three level model in four different implementation sites. They found that implementation of such a model lead to significant increase in student learning and overall school district performance. Additionally, they found that implementation of a three-level RTI model led to fewer students who were identified as having a learning disability and being in need of special education services. More students' needs were met in the general education setting before problems worsened and fewer students had to be considered for special education eligibility. Whether a school district chooses to implement a four-level RTI model or a three-level RTI model, the positive effects for students remain the same.

13
parental participation: the power of one

Parental participation is not the same as parental attendance. Parental attendance at school functions, PTO meetings, sporting events, parent-teacher meetings, etc., has been encouraged by educators for many decades. Parental participation has a more complex past. While parental attendance is a mandatory requirement, parental participation is encouraged. Regarding special education, parental participation was written into the original Public Law 94-142 (1975) as a part of the due process protections afforded to both student and parent. This included, among others, such rights as:

- prior notification regarding evaluation,

- need for parental permission for evaluation and placement,

- the right to contest and redress grievances through a due process hearing,

- to be given a parents' handbook of rights regarding special education procedures,

- and the right to participate as an equal member of IEP meetings should the student qualify to receive special education services.

These parental rights have served to both protect civil liberties and strongly encourage parental attendance at important meetings. Unfortunately, in spite of all the legal protections, the current "test and place" system for identifying special education students often puts the parent in the role of a "consent giver" with limited opportunity for participation. For instance, in most school districts currently using a traditional evaluation procedure, the parent is asked to participate in two meetings – first is the meeting to obtain parental permission for evaluation followed by a second meeting to discuss the results of that evaluation and special education services, if the student qualifies. This system would seem to promote a "consent giver" role for the parent and relegate parental "participation" to an exercise in compliance.

The RTI model has more room for parent participation due to its procedural sequence. In RTI, since the needs of the student are addressed first through general education interventions, there is more opportunity for parental participation. A typical procedural sequence in a RTI model would have at least eight meetings in which the parent is invited to participate as an equal member of a student study team. The parent's role would be to contribute information which only a parent would have – developmental and medical history, observations about behavior patterns around the home, details such as the amount of sleep on a nightly basis, interaction with siblings, ability to form friendships, amount of time devoted to homework, student's attitude towards teachers and school, and observed academic strengths and weaknesses. Notice that instead of a consent giver role, the parent in a RTI model is contributing information which only he or she knows. This contributed information will be only one of several areas or domains which the team will explore while attempting to determine and define the student's academic or behavioral difficulty.

Over a period of several meetings, the parent's participation and contribution can often be seen in the intervention decided on by the team. The parent may have a role in both the collection of baseline data and in the progress monitoring phase. Part of the intervention may take place in the home. Parental participation is further encouraged by the charting process, which clearly demonstrates whether or not the selected intervention is effective. Any parent can understand the logic of using a chart. The progress monitoring data are either going up, down, or remaining the same (flat-lining). This chart is where the student's response to intervention is recorded. It is a visual representation of how that student responded to an intervention designed to increase performance in a specific academic skill. Even better, the parent has had an expanded opportunity to both participate and contribute in a way meaningful to the him/her. Because of the parent's extended participation in the intervention process, should the intensity of the student's needs be more than the intensity of general education interventions available, it will not take the parent by surprise if the subject of special education services and placement occurs. Actually, in a RTI model, special education is not viewed as a "place" but as a more intensive intervention to meet the needs of the child. The need for the highest intensity of intervention is demonstrated by the chart which shows the student's lack of response to a data-based prescriptive intervention plan in a general education setting. If the parent(s) has participated in the intervention and progress monitoring parts of RTI, then he or she will readily understand why access to special education services may be a necessary step to assist the child.

Hopefully at this point you as a parent think that this RTI model sounds pretty good. But wait! What if you live in a place where RTI is being implemented? What if you have had nothing but negative experiences with your school district? What if your child is already in special education, but you feel there are problems and the district is non-responsive? What if you don't want your child tested for a disability because you are afraid your child might actually have a problem?

First, understand that your local school district has a legal obligation to initiate and promote what is referred to as "Child Find." This is the district's legal responsibility to find (identify) any student from birth to 21 years, 11 months, and 30 days who might qualify for and/or need specially designed services offered under any of 13 disability categories. This obligation covers not only the local public schools but also any private or parochial schools located in the district's attendance area. While it is true that parents can and sometimes do refer their child for an educational assessment through the school district, usually referrals come from teachers.

Second, understand that your due process rights (as mentioned earlier) are taken quite seriously by the school district. For instance, your giving permission for a district-initiated psycho-educational evaluation does not obligate you to give permission for special education placement, should your child qualify. If your child is already in special education and there is a dispute concerning an area such as discipline, re-evaluation, the child's individual education plan, etc, refer to the parents' handbook of rights you have been given at almost every meeting you ever attended. Your options and rights related to any dispute are spelled out in the handbook. Every state has some type of public advocacy assistance available without charge. This advocacy assistance can be useful in explaining to you what your rights are and what laws are applicable in your particular situation.

When disputes arise between parents and the district, especially concerning special education, there are two positions a parent can take. The first is a concerned but cooperative position that emphasizes the shared-responsibility relationship between school and parent. The goal here is improving communication so as not to sacrifice trust.

The second position is more adversarial. Trust between the parent and school has been lost. As a result, each meeting becomes a prolonged dispute as one side attacks and the other side defends. Having been to more meetings of this type than I care to admit, I must say that about halfway through such a meeting I find myself wondering, "But what about the child?" It seems that when relations between school and parent are permitted to deteriorate to the point that every meeting has to have an advocate or attorney and each meeting has to be tape recorded and later transcribed, then the educational needs of the student in question quickly become lost and the child is the loser. In this scenario, both school and parent have lost sight of what both wanted from the beginning – positive educational outcomes which produce a citizen prepared to take advantage of life's opportunities.

I would argue that if a dispute or difference of opinion should develop, please take position number one above. You may not realize it but you always have the power in this relationship. You may think you need an army to help you, but you don't really. Federal law has already given you ample rights and protections. You are the parent and your child is ultimately your joy and your responsibility. You have the right to say *yes* or *no* in educational matters. Any school will want your child to be successful and will generally go to great lengths to provide whatever educational assistance he or she needs.

14
it takes special people

The purpose of this book is not to degrade or belittle special education personnel. It takes a *special* person to work in the field of special education. The problems with special education and the special education eligibility determination process discussed in this book are not a result of the shortcomings of special education personnel. Rather, they are the results of the inadequate tools that special education personnel have been given, namely achievement tests, IQ tests, and the discrepancy model. Special educators are some of the brightest, most empathetic, and hardest-working people I have ever met. If it is true that the measure of a life is not in what you do, but in what you do for others, then there is a special place reserved in the afterlife for special educators. If it is also true that your profession or life's activity picks you instead of you picking it, then special educators are what is special about special education.

A representative sample of such professionals would include special education administrators and teachers, school psychologists, speech/language therapists, occupational therapists, physical therapists, and behavior specialists. They work daily in a climate of legal accountability and elevated expectations. The state and federal regulations governing the field of special education are numerous, unyielding, and often confusing. Yet, in spite of the litigious times we live in, special education professionals return each day determined to make a difference in each student's academic life. When concerned and caring parents accept their role of working with the school in a shared-responsibility effort, the result is a significant advance in promoting positive educational outcomes for all students.

Examples of how special educators are special people are plentiful; however, there are two that I would like to share with you. The following two stories capture the spirit of special educators and the dedication that they have to the children with which they work.

The first is about a man named Charles. Charles is now forty-nine years old. He grew up in Long Island, New York. Growing up, Charles was normal in most respects with one exception: he would not talk. It's not that he couldn't talk – he just would not talk. (This situation is now referred to as selective mutism and is often misidentified and/or confused with other disorders.) When Charles was still quite young, his parents were informed that Charles was, in all likelihood, mentally disabled and that the long-term prospects for Charles were pretty dismal. The general medical consensus at the time was that Charles might be able to earn a living working in one of the nearby factories—someday—maybe.

Charles explained many years later that he had a terrible stuttering problem. This speech/language problem caused great embarrassment and extreme self-consciousness when he attempted to talk. His school-aged peers laughed at Charles and ridiculed him for the way he talked. The result was that Charles did not seriously attempt to hold conversational speech until he was twenty-one years old. Today, Charles has three master's degrees and is working on his doctorate. He works in special education as a Behavior Specialist and is generally considered to be a truly gifted professional. His work with students who are experiencing behavioral and emotional difficulties is characterized by a well-developed sense of empathy, along with a strong dose of caring for the individual and the individual's family. Where Charles is now is a long way from the factories predicted so many years ago. Maybe your life activity *does* pick you, after all.

The second story is about David. His struggles make a truly remarkable story. David was born in North Carolina and seemed to be developing at a typical pace until age three when it was noted by his parents that his speech was seriously delayed. By age five or six he had some speech, but David was difficult to understand due to the number of articulation errors. He omitted and substituted certain consonant sounds that made his speaking hard to comprehend. His mother arranged for David to receive speech therapy. (These services were not available in public schools at that time.) The therapy was provided at a clinic many miles away, and the bi-weekly trip for several years was a major commitment of time and resources – resources not in great abundance. In the space of three years, David's mother had lost her forearm to cancer, along with her father and her husband. She was trying to raise David and two older siblings on a secretary's salary in the mid-1950s. Additionally, David's vision was terrible. After his first three years of bumping into everything, an eye exam indicated that David was close to being legally blind. So from about age four, he wore glasses with very thick lenses.

When David was eleven, he was diagnosed as having a rare genetic disorder known as Marfan's Syndrome. The diagnosis helped explain why David was so thin and tall, why his heart was located to the right, not the left, why he had flat feet, why he was double-jointed everywhere possible, and why he was so physically unco-ordinated. He had many things going against him – many things, but not every-thing. He was good in math and reading; poor in spelling and writing. He loved gardening and tinkering with mechanical objects. David was teased and ridiculed all of his life because he was different. Young children don't understand "different" and adults are uncomfortable around it. But through it all, one thing became very apparent. Over time, David learned to accept himself and his condition. In doing so, he accepted others who were also different. In a crowd, he would always gravitate to those individuals he thought to be in worse shape than himself and they became his friends. (This level of self-acceptance is a point of focus in the popular children's book entitled *You Are Special* by Max Lucado.)

David attended a small liberal arts college and majored in education—specifically, special education. He was in his senior year and doing his "practice" teaching in a nearby school district when he suffered from an aneurysm and died suddenly. David had said on more than one occasion that he felt at ease when working with special education students because he was recognized by the students as being "one of them". There was a level of acceptance for him that was not to be found in general society. He died on an emergency room gurney just seconds after being asked by the attending physician what he was going to do after college graduation. The last words he ever uttered were, "I am going to be a special education teacher." A curious postscript to this story is that David's older siblings both went into the field of education – one as a history teacher and the other in special education.

What makes special education special? People like Charles and David and the thousands of special educators throughout the United States. Both Charles and David had to overcome problems most of us will never have to endure. They demonstrated that through the effort to improve others, you improve yourself. By assisting those in need of assistance, you assist all. By looking for new and innovative methods to provide assistive educational services, meeting students' needs, and avoiding the practice of labeling students, the educational community is moving slowly towards a better and brighter day. This better and brighter day will emphasize more effective assistance provided in general education, will provide a self-correcting model that eliminates any doubt as to whether or not learning is taking place and, most importantly, if special education is deemed necessary, it will not be seen as a "place" but rather a continuum point representing a higher intensity of intervention. The move from the traditional model to an RTI model will be facilitated if parents work with the local school district. Response to intervention has much to offer education. Reluctance to change and difficulty of acceptance will be two major hurdles to leap. Through collaborative and constructive efforts, it is hoped that a new day for your child and all students is close at hand.

The key is giving educators the tools to make implementation of an RTI model successful. It is not as simple as proclaiming that you are now using RTI. There are a few prerequisites to RTI implementation. Some of the prerequisites are conceptual and some are applied activities. First, all those involved in implementation must possess a certain mind-set and educational philosophy. The chart which follows details the necessary mind-set and philosophy.

Second, all those involved in implementation must receive a significant amount of training. In the state of North Carolina, five school districts were selected by the Department of Public Instruction to take part in a RTI pilot study. Prior to implementation, the educators in those five districts received twenty-one days of training. These twenty-one days were spread over an entire school year. Topics covered in those trainings included: how to conduct a local norming project, curriculum-based assessments, team building exercises, how to implement the problem-solving model, research-based interventions for reading, research-based interventions for math, research-based interventions for written expression, research based interventions for behavioral difficulties, progress monitoring, charting, IEP development, and RTI case studies. A significant amount of time is required just to give the personnel the skills necessary for implementation. Those school districts are also being provided with follow-up trainings as needed, opportunities for discussion and sharing of ideas during implementation, and oversight.

A third prerequisite is the local norming project. (The benefits of using local norms were discussed in chapter eight.) Again, this is a year-long process. While the school districts in NC were receiving training, they were also performing CBM assessments with students in the districts to collect the norm (or typical score) for students in those districts on various academic skills, in various grade levels, for fall, winter, and spring. Thus, at the end of the year, each school district had their own norms and these norms were combined to form a set of NC state norms. After a year of preparation, these school districts possessed the mindset, philosophy, skills, and tools necessary to make RTI implementation successful. This teaches us that RTI implementation is not something to be taken lightly. It requires a significant investment of time and resources. Still, the benefits provided to the students through implementation make it seem like a small price to pay.

Required Changes in Mind-Set and Philosophy

Changes in mind-set that are necessary for all of those involved:	Changes in philosophy that are necessary for all of those involved:
Student problems can be defined and changed	All children can learn
Questions drive assessments	Educators are responsible to meet the needs of all children
Enabled learning rather than discrepancy or diagnosis is the goal	Parents possess a wealth of knowledge about their children and should be partners in the educational system
Intervention is derived from analysis of baseline data	Solutions and strategies are best identified when educators, parents, and others involved work collaboratively
	Proactive instruction should be provided within general education setting, so children are assisted before concerns arise
	Prevention is more cost- effective than remediation
	Children's needs should be met in the general education setting whenever appropriate
	Teachers and parents deserve the resources necessary to meet the educational needs of all children
	Best educational strategy is one that works
	Effectiveness of educational strategies must be evaluated frequently
	Accurate information about student progress should be communicated regularly
	Educational system must provide opportunities for all children to achieve their goals

15
coming full circle

This book began with a story about a little boy who was failed by the traditional system and me in several ways. In that story, I wrote about the questions posed to me about the traditional system by the student's teacher and mother. That was a very challenging meeting, and I was involved in several meetings like that while I was working in the traditional discrepancy model. Since then, I have taken the journey detailed in this book, a journey from theoretical darkness to enlightened application. Research and implementation experience have shown us the fallacies of the traditional model and that there is a better way to go about meeting the needs of students.

I spend a lot of my time now training state departments, school districts, and individual schools on how to implement a Response to Intervention (RTI) model. I also work as a school psychologist in a school district in North Carolina that made the switch from the traditional discrepancy model to a Response to Intervention model. I now have the pleasure of sitting in on a different type of meetings. These are meetings in which through the RTI process a student's needs have been specifically identified and addressed. School staff and parents are seeing the students make progress, and the students are reaping the benefits. I would like to detail the story of one of these students. Her name is Kalie, and her story is a wonderful tribute to what a Response to Intervention model can do for children in need:

I was walking out of a school building one day when a lady walked up to me and asked me if I was Tom Jenkins. I had spent a great deal of time at this school the previous school year training staff involved in the implementation of RTI. This school year I was providing some implementation oversight. I met with them periodically to provide advice, answer questions, provide encouragement, and provide any follow-up training to polish their previously learned skills. After confirming that I was indeed who she thought, this woman began to thank me for what I had done for her daughter, Kalie.

She told me that her family had moved to Wilmington two years ago from New York. Kalie had attended kindergarten, first, and second grade in New York. When Kalie was in first grade this mother and her husband began to realize that there was something wrong with Kalie's reading. Despite requesting that Kalie receive some assistance with her reading, no extra help was provided. The teachers told her "not to worry that there was no problem." When Kalie entered the second grade, things became worse. Because of her reading difficulties she was starting to become very frustrated with school. Her anxiety level about going to school was so high that she began crying and often times throwing up in the mornings before school. Kalie's self-confidence plummeted, and it began affecting all aspects of her life.

Kalie's parents again went to the school and requested help. The school recommended an evaluation to determine if Kalie was eligible to receive special education services. Kalie's mother stated that no prior remedial services were provided. There was no attempt to correct the problem within the general education setting. If Kalie was to receive any help, that help had to come in the form of special education services. That was the only option presented to Kalie's parents, so that is where they placed their hopes.

At the time New York used the traditional discrepancy model. Not surprisingly, knowing what you now know about traditional discrepancy model, Kalie did not qualify for special education services. Kalie's mother became emotional when she stated that the school told her that Kalie's achievement scores were too high for her to qualify for help. Her mother found herself thinking that Kalie's problems needed to be worse and that she needed to fail to get the help that she needed.

Following that evaluation Kalie seemed to get pushed to the side. Kalie's mother commented that because of the school tax in New York, Kalie's school was a big beautiful state-of-the-art facility. However, she felt that because her daughter did not fit into a category, she was just forgotten within that lovely facility. The irony was overwhelming. For the remainder of second grade Kalie's reading problem worsened, and by the end of the school year her self-confidence had been destroyed.

That summer Kalie's father received a job opportunity in North Carolina and the family had to make the move. Kalie's mother said that she remembered school staff at Kalie's school in New York telling her that she would be very unhappy with the schools in North Carolina. They told her that the difference between the schools in New York and North Carolina was like night and day. She stated that thankfully, for Kalie's sake, they were right; however, the difference was not like night and day, but like discrepancy model versus RTI.

Kalie entered the third grade in North Carolina, and in the first week her teacher called her parents to voice her concerns about Kalie's reading skills. This initiated level one of the problem-solving model. The teacher met with Kalie's parents and showed her data that she had collected concerning Kalie's reading skills. Her parents were staggered to find out that Kalie was reading on a first grade, first month level (1.1). Kalie's mother shared that she and Kalie shed a lot of tears that night, and that the school began tutoring services immediately.

At the end of level one, Kalie was still struggling so they decided to send the case on to level two. At level two Kalie's parents began meeting with Kalie's teacher, the third grade level team, and the school counselor. A level two, intervention plan was created. Kalie began receiving instruction from a reading recovery teacher, small group instruction in the classroom, reading kindergarten level books (in an attempt to increase her fluency and self-confidence), and sending home books the night before they were to be read in class. Following implementation of the level two interventions, Kalie's parents and her teacher did see some improvement in reading; she was now reading on a second grade second month level (2.2). Kalie still struggled with reading, and there was no improvement in her self-esteem.

Because of the experience that Kalie's parents had in New York they believed that special education was the answer. For that reason, following the completion of level two they requested that Kalie be evaluated again using the discrepancy model. The school staff reluctantly granted their wish. Not surprisingly the results were the same. Kalie's achievement scores were not low enough for her to show a discrepancy and receive special education services. But where in the traditional model her case would have been dropped at this point, there were options still available to her in the RTI model. Her case became a level three case, and Kalie's parents began working with the school's Student Support Team.

As part of level three of the problem-solving model process, school staff began administering CBE assessments with Kalie to collect data to identify her specific strengths and weaknesses in reading. Through this assessment they were able to identify that Kalie needed instruction in phonemic awareness (understanding the sounds that letters make and how to blend and segment those sounds) and decoding (how to sound out words). Kalie began receiving intervention instruction in these areas from trained staff for 20 minutes a day, three days a week. She also began receiving instruction in those areas one-on-one from the school counselor. Kalie also began looping into other third grade classes during the day so that she could receive reading instruction twice a day. All the while, her mom was given activities to do with her at home to work on phonemic awareness, blending, and segmenting.

During this intervention plan progress monitoring data were collected using the CBE assessments to ensure that Kalie was making the progress that they wanted to see. If progress was not seen, adjustments were made to the interventions in an attempt to create more progress. Her progress monitoring data were charted by the team so that a visual representation of her skill acquisition could be shared with school staff and Kalie's parents. This mother stated that the team was working to make things better for her child. "They were very giving of themselves." She went on to say that the school staff showed through their actions that they wanted what was best for Kalie. That is nice to hear, but I wanted to know about Kalie. What did the data show after interventions?

She then began to share with me the most amazing part of this story. As a result of the data-based prescriptive interventions coupled with the adjustments made through progress monitoring, Kalie's progress was incredible. By the spring of her third grade year, Kalie was reading over a hundred words per minute and on a fourth grade level (4.0)! Additionally, when Kalie took the state standards-based reading test at the end of the third grade, she received a score of 4 out of 4, which is the highest possible score. This is remarkable considering that Kalie's mother confided that she and her husband had considered third grade retention for Kalie just a few months before. She continued to explain that the effects were more than just academic. Kalie's self-esteem improved by leaps and bounds. Now she socializes with a group of kids who read and compare books and compete against each other for Accelerated Reading points. Her mother stated, "Through the RTI process the school staff did so much for Kalie and for us. I left a lot of those meetings very emotional, but it was wonderful. *It was the most wonderful thing that anyone has ever done for my child."*

Kalie's mother then reflected on the frustrations of the past with the discrepancy model. She explained that she was furious in New York. She felt like they did nothing for Kalie there, and she would like so much to go back and show them the RTI process and tell them that this is the way that it should be done. She still wonders to this day how school staff could have just let Kalie's reading problems go. Kalie's mother stated, **"Every child deserves RTI; no child should be left behind like Kalie was in New York."** She further explained that the school staff in North Carolina, through the RTI model, did more for Kalie in less than a year than the school staff in New York did in three years. I explained to her that it was not the fault of the school staff in New York. They were merely using the flawed tools that they had been provided. She became agitated at that point and said that all school systems needed to find the funding to make RTI happen for all kids.

Kalie's parents are experiencing some additional positive experiences from having gone through the RTI process with school staff. She explained that she and her husband have a special warm feeling for the staff at Kalie's school. She feels like they worked together to achieve a goal, and through that process they created a bond. She stated that Kalie could not be where she is today without the school staff and the RTI process. Kalie needed them and they were there for her. Through the RTI process they went above and beyond the traditional model to help Kalie. Now, whenever they go to the school, they feel like they are going to see friends.

At a later time I had the chance to meet Kalie. Standing before me was a tall, long dark haired, beautiful young lady who exuded self-confidence. When I asked her about the RTI process, she said initially that it was "cool and fun." She enjoyed getting all of the help, taking the CBEs, and charting her progress. But then I pressed her for more information. A big smile spread across her face, and she asked, "Did you know that I can read big books now?" I responded that her mom had told me that. "I am doing better," she said, "and I feel good about myself." Isn't that what it is all about?

Glossary

Curriculum Based Evaluation – (CBE) assessment tools derived directly from the curriculum that the student is expected to learn. This is one of the components of a Response to Intervention model. Similar terms are curriculum based measurement (CBM) and curriculum based assessment (CBA).

Blends – The sound that a couple or group of letters make. For example the sound that *sh*, ch, or *ck* make.

Discrepancy Model – The traditional model used to identify a student as having a learning disability. In this mode, the student's intelligence (IQ) is compared to his/her academic achievement scores to see if there is a significant difference. If there is a significant discrepancy, an achievement score is significantly below the IQ, then the student can be identified as a student with a learning disability.

Individuals with Disabilities in Education Act – (IDEA) A federal law that was originally written in 1975 with the purpose of making education more accessible to students with disabilities. It has since been rewritten in increase the number of students that it covers and improve services provided to those students.

Intelligence – (IQ) A theoretical construct. It is believed to be a person's level of ability or level of potential.

Learning Disabled – (LD) A theoretical idea based on the traditional line of reasoning. If a person has an academic skill that is significant below their theoretical level of ability, then some believe that is indicative of a learning disability that academic area.

Phonemes – The sounds that letters make.

Problem Solving Model – (PSM) A seven step cyclical model of analysis that is similar to a scientific model. This is one of the components of a Response to Intervention model.

Progress Monitor – To monitor the progress of a student. In an RTI model a student's progress should be monitored two to three times a week, and the data collected should be used to make decisions about what and how to teach the child.

Response To Intervention – (RTI) a model for matching intervention resources to the intensity of a student's academic need. The model is comprised of a problem-solving model combined with curriculum-based evaluation. The student's learning rate over time and level of performance are used to make instructional decisions.

Sight Words – Being able to identify words quickly just by sight recognition.

References

American Psychiatric Association. (2000). *Diagnostic and statistical manual of mental disorders* (Fourth Edition - Text Revised). Washington, DC: Author.

Armbruster, B.B., Stevens, R.G., & Rosenshine, B. (1977). *Analyzing content coverage and emphasis: A study of three curricula and two tests* (Technical Representative N26). Urbana, IL: University of Illinois, Center for the Study of Reading.

Beck, R., Conrad, D., & Anderson, P. (1997). *Basic Skill Builders.* Longmont, Colorado: Sopris West.

Braden, J.P. (1997). The practical impact of intellectual assessment issues. *School* Psychology Review, 26(2), 242-248.

Burns, M., Appleton, J., & Stehouwer J. (2006). *Meta-analytic review of responsiveness-to-intervention research: Examining field-based and research-implemented models.* Manuscript submitted for publication.

California Department of Education. (1994). *California learning assessment system: State results.* Sacramento, CA: Author.

Christenson, S.L. , & Sheridan, S.M. (2001). *Schools and Families-Creating Essential Connections for Learning.* New York: The Guildford Press

Clarizio, H.F. & Bennett, D.E. (1987). Diagnostic utility of the K-ABC and WISC-R/PIAT in determining severe discrepancy. *Psychology in the Schools, 24,* 309-315.

Colarusso, R.P., Keel, M.C., & Dangel, H.L. (2001). A comparison of eligibility criteria and their impact on minority representation in LD programs. *Learning Disabilities Research and Practice, 16(1),* 1-7.

Coles, G.S. (1978). The learning disabilities test battery: Empirical and social issues. *Harvard Educational Review, 48,* 313-340.

Cone, T.E. & Wilson, L.R. (1981). Quantifying a severe discrepancy: A critical analysis. *Learning Disability Quarterly, 4,* 359-371.

Deno, S. (1985). Curriculum-based measurement: The emerging alternative. *Exceptional Children, 52(3),* 219-232.

Deno, S., Marston, D., & Mirkin, P. (1982). Valid measurement procedures for continuous evaluation of written expression. *Exceptional Children, 48,* 368-371.

Deno, S., Marston, D., Shinn, M., & Tindal, G. (1983). Oral reading fluency: A simple datum for scaling reading disability. *Topics in Learning and Learning Disability, 2,* 53-59.

Deno, S., Marston, D., & Tindal, G. (1985). Direct and frequent curriculum-based measurement: An alternative for educational decision making. *Special Services in the Schools, 2,* 5-28.

Deno, S. & Mirkin, P. (1977). *Data-based program modification: A manual.* Reston, Virginia. Council for Exceptional Children.

Deno, S., Mirkin, P., & Chiang, B. (1982). Identifying valid measures of reading. *Exceptional Children, 49,* 36-45.

Deno, S., Mirkin, P., Chiang, B., & Lowry, L. (1980). *Relationships among simple measures of reading and performance on standardized achievement tests* (Research Report No. 20). Minneapolis, Minnesota. University of Minnesota, Institute for Research on Learning Disabilities.

Don't rely on aptitude/achievement to diagnose learning disabilities (2000, March). *Today's School Psychologist, (3)*8, 10.

Dwyer, K. (2001, February). School Psychologists: Innovators or bean counters?. *Communique,* 21.

Elliott, S.N. & Fuchs, L.S. (1997). The utility of curriculum-based measurement and performance assessment as alternatives to traditional intelligence and achievement tests. *School Psychology Review, 26(2),* 224-233.

Espin, C.A., Busch, T.W., Shin, J., & Kruschwitz, R. (2001). Curriculum-based measurement in the content areas: Validity of vocabulary-matching as an indicator of performance in social studies. *Learning Disabilities Research and Practice, 16(3),* 142-151.

Esters, I.G., Ittenbach, R.F., & Han, K. (1997). Today's IQ tests: Are they better than their historical predecessors? *School Psychology Review, 26(2),* 211-224.

Evans, J.H., Carlsen, R.N., & McGrew, K.S. (1993). Classification of exceptional students with the Woodcock-Johnson Psycho-Educational Battery-Revised [Monograph Series: WJ-R Monograph]. *Journal of Psychoeducational Assessment,* 6-19.

Fletcher, J.M., Francis, D., Shaywitz, S., Lyon, G.R., Foorman, B.R., Stuebing, K.K., & Shaywitz, B. (1998). Intelligent testing and the discrepancy model for children with learning disabilities. *Learning Disabilities Research & Practice, 13,* 186-203.

Foegen, A. & Deno, S.L. (2001). Identifying growth indicators for low-achieving students in middle school mathematics. *The Journal of Special Education, 35,* 4-16.

Foorman, B.R., Francis, D.J., Fletcher, J.M., Schatschneider, C., & Mehta, P. (1998). The role of instruction in learning to read: Preventing reading failure in at-risk-children. *Journal of Educational Psychology, 90,* 38-57.

Fuchs, L.S.., Deno, S.L., & Mirkin, P.K. (1984). The effects of frequent curriculum-based measurement and evaluation on pedagogy, student achievement, and student awareness of learning. *American educational Research Journal, 21(2),* 449-460.

Fuchs, L.S. & Fuchs, D. (1984). Criterion-referenced assessment without measurement: How accurate for special education? *Remedial and Special Education, 5(4),* 29-32.

Fuchs, L.S. & Fuchs, D. (1997). Use of curriculum-based measurement in identifying students with disabilities. *Focus On Exceptional Children, 30(3),* 1-15.

Fuchs, L.S. & Fuchs, D. (1999). Performance assessment using complex tasks: Implications for children with high-incidence disabilities. In R. Gallimore, L.P. Bernheimer, D.L.

MacMillan, D.L. Speece, & S. Vaughn (Eds.), *Developmental perspectives on children with high-incidence disabilities* (pp.199-220). Mahwah, New Jersey: Lawrence Erlbaum Associates.

Fuchs, D., Fuchs, L.S., Benowitz, S., & Barringer, K., (1987). Norm-referenced tests: Are they valid for use with handicapped students? *Exceptional Children, 54(3)*, 263-271.

Fuchs, L.S., Fuchs, D., & Hamlett, C.L. (1989). Effects of instrumental use of curriculum-based measurement to enhance instructional programs. *Remedial & Special Education, 10(2)*, 43-52.

Fuchs, L.S., Fuchs, D., Hamlett, C.L., & Allinder, R.M. (1991). The contribution of skills analysis to curriculum-based measurement in spelling. *Exceptional Children, 57*, 443-452.

Fuchs, L.S., Fuchs, D., Hamlett, C.L., Phillips, N.B., & Bentz, J. (1994). Classwide curriculum-based measurement: Helping general educators meet the challenge of student diversity. *Exceptional Children, 60(6)*, 518-537.

Fuchs, L.S., Fuchs, D., Hamlett, C.L., & Stecker, P.M. (1991). Effects of curriculum-based measurement and consultation on teacher planning and student achievement in mathematics operations. *American Educational Research Journal, 28*, 617-641.

Fuchs, L.S., Fuchs, D., & Warren, L. (1982). *Special education practice in evaluating student progress toward goals* (Research Report No. 21). Minneapolis: University of Minnesota, Instutute for Research on Learning Disabilities.

Galagan, J.E. (1986). Psychoeducational testing: Turn out the lights, the party's over. *Exceptional Children, 52*, 288-298.

Germann, G. & Tindal, G. (1985). An application of curriculum-based assessment: The use of direct and repeated measurement. *Exceptional Children, 52*, 244-265.

Gottlieb, J., Alter, M., Gottlieb, B.M., & Wishner, J. (1994). Speical education in urban America: It's not justifiable for many. *Journal of Special Education, 27*, 453-465.

Gresham, F.M., MacMillan, D.L., & Bocian, K.M. (1996). Learning disabilities, low achievement, and mild mental retardation: More alike than different? *Journal of Learning Disabilities, 29*, 570-581.

Hall, T.E. (1998). District-wide strategy to monitor the placement and performance of students from ethnically diverse populations: A case study. *Diagnostique, 23(3),* 141-166.

Hamayan, E.V. & Damico, J.S. (1991). *Limiting bias in the assessment of bilingual students.* Austin: Pro-Ed.

Heller, K., Holtzman, and Messick, N. (1982). National Research Council Special Task Force Report, Washington, DC: National Academy Press.

Howell, K.W. & Nolet, V. (2000). *Curriculum-based evaluation: Teaching and decision making.* Belmont: Wadsworth Thomson Learning.

Jenkins, J.R., Deno, S.L., & Mirkin, P.K. (1979). Measuring pupil progress toward the least restrictive alternative. *Learning Disability Quarterly, 2,* 81-91.

Jenkins, J.R., Jewell, M., Leceister, N., Jenkins, L., & Troutner, N. (1990). *Development of a school building model for education of handicapped and at risk students in general education classrooms.* Paper presented at the annual meeting of the American Educational Research Association, Boston, MA.

Jenkins, T. (2002). *Generalizability study on local norms using curriculum based measurement.* Manuscript submitted for publication.

Jensen, A. (1980). *Bias in Mental Testing.* New York: Free Press.

Jones, E.D. & Krouse, J.P. (1988). The effectiveness of data-based instruction by student teachers in classrooms for pupils with mild handicaps. *Teacher Education and Special Education, 11(1),* 9-19.

Kamphaus, R.W., Frick, P.J., & Lahey, B.B. (1991). Methodological issues in learning disabilities diagnosis in clinical populations. *Journal of Learning Disabilities, 24,* 613-618.

Kaufman, A.S. (1994). *Intelligent Testing with the WISC-III.* New York: Wiley.

Kavale, K.A. & Forness, S.R. (2001). Discrepancy models and the meaning of learning disability. In T.E. Scruggs & M.A. Mastropieri (Eds.) *Advances in Learning and Behavioral Disabilities Volume 15: Technological Applications* (pp.187-235). New York: Elsevier.

Laut, M., Lilly, R., Barbour, B., & Jenkins, T. (2001). Rule Replacements Pilot Project. Unpublished report and raw data.

Lichtenstein, R. (2002). Learning disabilities criteria: Recommendations for change in IDEA reauthorization. *Communique, 30(6),* 1-3.

Lopez, R. (1997). The practical impact of current research issues in intelligence test interpretation and use for multicultural populations. *School Psychology Review, 26(2),* 249-254.

Lucado, M. (1997). *You Are Special.* Wheaton , ILL: Crossway Books

Macmann, G.M., Barnett, D.W., Lombard, T.J., Belton-Kocher, E., & Sharpe, M.N. (1989). On the actuarial classification of children: Fundamental studies of classification agreement. *Journal of Special Education, 23,* 127-143.

MacMillan, D.L., Gresham, F.M., & Bocian, K.M. (1998). Discrepancy between definitions of learning disabilities and school practices: An empirical investigation. *Journal of Learning Disabilities, 31,* 314-326.

Magnusson, D. (1984). *An analysis of the effect of different peer performance discrepancy decision rules on the proportion of elementary students determined eligible for special education assessment in reading and math.* Unpublished doctoral dissertation, University of Minnesota, Minneapolis.

Marston, D.B. (1989). A curriculum-based measurement approach to assessing academic performance: What it is and why do it. In M.R. Shinn (Ed.), *Curriculum-based measurement: Assessing special children* (pp.18-78). New York: Guilford.

Marston, D. & Deno, S.L. (1982). *Implementation of direct and repeated measurement in the school setting* (Research Report No. 106). Minneapolis, Minnesota: University of Minnesota, Institute for Research on Learning Disabilities.

Marston, D., Deno, S.L., & Tindal, G. (1983). *A comparison of standardized achievement tests and direct measurement techniques in measuring pupil progress* (Research Report No. 126). Minneapolis, Minnesota: University of Minnesota, Institute for Research on Learning Disabilities.

Marston, D. & Magnusson, D. (1985). Implementing curriculum-based measurement in special and regular education settings. *Exceptional Children, 52,* 266-276.

Marston, D. & Magnusson, D. (1988). Curriculum-based measurement: District level implementation. In J.L. Graden, J.E. Zins, & M.J. Curtis (Eds.), *Alternative Educational Delivery Systems: Enhancing Instructional Options for All Students* (pp. 137-172). Washington, DC: National Association of School Psychologists.

Marston, D., Mirkin, P., & Deno, S.L. (1984). Curriculum-based measurement: An alternative to traditional screening, referral, and identification of learning disabled students. *Journal of Special Education, 18,* 109-118.

Marston, D., Tindal, G., & Deno, S.L. (1982). *Predictive efficiency of direct repeated measurement : An analysis of cost and accuracy in classification* (Research Report No. 104). Minneapolis, Minnesota: University of Minnesota, Institute for Research on Learning Disabilities.

Marston, D., Tindal, G., & Deno, S.L. (1984). Eligibility for learning disability services: A direct and repeated measurement approach. *Exceptional Children, 50,* 554-555.

Mirkin, P. (1980). Conclusions. In J. Ysseldyke & M. Thurlow (Eds.) *The special education assessment and decision-making process: Seven (see studies).* Minneapolis: University of Minnesota Institute for Research in Learning Disabilities.

Mirkin, P., Deno, S., Tindal, G., & Kuehnle, K (1982). Frequency of measurement and data utilization strategies as factors in standardized behavior assessment of academic skill. *Journal of Behavioral Assessment, 4(4),* 361-370.

National Coalition of Advocates for Students. (1985). Barriers to Excellence: Out Children at Risk.

Oakland, T. & Matuszek, P. (1977). Using tests in a non-discriminatory fashion. In T. Oakland (Ed.), *Psychological and educational assessment of minority children* (pp.52-69). New York: Bruner-Mazel.

Popham, W.J. (1999). Where large scale educational assessment is heading and why it shouldn't. *Educational Measurement: Implications and Practice, 18,* 13-17.

Reschley, D. (1996). Identification and assessment of students with disabilities. *Special Education for Students with Disabilities, 6,* 40-53.

Salmon-Cox, L. (1981). Teachers and standardized achievement tests: What's really happening? *Phi Delta Kappan, 62(9),* 631-634.

Salvia, J., & Ysseldyke, J. (1985). *Assessment in special and remedial education.* Boston: Houghton Mifflin.

Schenck, B., Fitzsimmons, J., Bullard, P.C., Taylor, H.G., & Satz, P. (1980). A prevention model for children at risk for reading failure. In R.M. Knights & D.J. Bakker (Eds.). *Treatment of hyperactive and learning disordered children* (pp. 31-48). Baltimore: University Park Press.

Scriven, M. (1983). Comments on gene class. *Policy Studies Review, 2,* 79-85.

Share, D.L., McGee, R., & Silva, P.D. (1989). IQ and reading progress: A test of the capacity notion of IQ. *Journal of the American Academic of Child and Adolescent Psychiatry, 28,* 97-100.

Shinn, M.R. (1988). Development of curriculum-based local norms for use in special education decision making. *School Psychology Review, 17(1), 61-80.*

Shinn, M.R. & Marston, D. (1985). Differentiating mildly handicapped, low-achieving, and regular education students: A curriculum-based approach. *Remedial and Special Education, 6,* 31-45.

Shinn, M.R., Tindal, G.A., Spira, D., & Marston, D. (1987). Practice of learning disabilities as social policy. *Learning Disability Quarterly, 10,* 17-28.

Shinn, M.R., Tindal, G.A., & Stein, S. (1988). Curriculum-based measurement and the identification of mildly handicapped students: A research review. *Professional School Psychology, 3(1),* 69-85.

Shinn, M.R., Ysseldyke, J., Deno, S., & Tindal, G. (1982). *A comparison of psychometric and functional differences between students labeled learning disabled and low achieving* (Research Report No. 71). Minneapolis, Minnesota. University of Minnesota, Institute for Research on Learning Disabilities.

Shinn, M.R., Ysseldyke, J., Deno, S., & Tindal, G. (1986). A comparison of differences between students labeled learning disabled and low achieving on measures of classroom performance. *Journal of Learning Disabilities, 19,* 545-552.

Siegel, L.S. (1989). IQ is irrelevant to the definition of learning disabilities. *Journal of Learning Disabilities, 22,* 469-478.

Sinclair, E. & Alexson, J. (1986). Learning Disability Discrepancy Formulas: Similarities and differences among them. *Learning Disabilities Research, 1(2),* 112-118.

Smith, D.R. (2000, Spring). Data-based decision making and accountability in today's schools. Assessment Focus, 9(1), 1-2.

Thorndike, R.L. (1963). *The Concepts of Over and Under Achievement.* New York: Teachers College, Columbia University Press.

Tindal, G., Germann, G., & Deno, S. (1983). *Descriptive research on the Pine County norms: A compilation of findings* (Research Report No. 132). Minneapolis, Minnesota: University of Minnesota, Institute for Research on Learning Disabilities.

Torgeson, J.K. (1997). The prevention and remediation of reading disabilities: Evaluating what we know from research. Journal of Academic Language Therapy, 1, 11-47.

United States Office of Education. (1984). *Seventh annual report to Congress on the implementation of Public Law 94-142*. Washington, DC: Author.

Vellutino, F., Scanlon, D., & Lyon, R. (2000). Differentiating between difficult-to-remediate and readily remediated poor readers. *Journal of Learning Disabilities, 33,* 223-238.

Warner, M., Schumaker, J., Alley, G., & Deshler, D. (1980). Learning disabled adolescents in the public schools: Are they different from other low achievers. *Exceptional Eduction Quarterly, 1,* 217-236.

White, W.J. & Wigle, S.E. (1986). Patterns of discrepancy over time as revealed by a standard-score comparison formula. *Learning Disabilities Research, 2(1),* 14-20.

Ysseldyke, J., Algozzine, B., Shinn, M., & McGue, M. (1979). *Similarities and differences* between low achievers and students labeled learning disabled: Identical twins with *different mothers* (Research Report No. 13). Minneapolis, Minnesota: University of Minnesota, Institute for Research on Learning Disabilities.

Ysseldyke, J., Dawson, P., Lehr, C., Reschly, D., Reynolds, M., & Telzrow, C. (1997). *School Psychology: A Blueprint for Training and Practice*. Bethesda, MD: National Association of School Psychologists.

It is not who is right, but what is right that is of importance

-Thomas H. Huxley

Printed in the United States
127630LV00003B/307-333/A

9 781599 320311